WITHDRAWN

FIRST
IMPRESSIONS

FIRST IMPRESSIONS

ESSAYS ON POETRY, CRITICISM, AND PROSODY

BY LLEWELLYN JONES

Essay Index Reprint Series

BOOKS FOR LIBRARIES PRESS
FREEPORT, NEW YORK

First Published 1925
Reprinted 1968

LIBRARY OF CONGRESS CATALOG CARD NUMBER:
68-29222

PRINTED IN THE UNITED STATES OF AMERICA

TO SUSAN WARREN WILBUR

Associate editor and associate everything else

Contents

I

II

III

FIRST
IMPRESSIONS

Edwin Arlington Robinson

EDWIN ARLINGTON ROBINSON was the poet of an audience fit and few until the publication of his collected works, the fruit of twenty-five years, in 1921. In that year he received the so-called Pulitzer prize (Pulitzer himself did not provide for an award for poetry), and the tide of public recognition set in. Mr. Robinson has never been a facile writer and frequent publisher, the collected poems of a quarter-century filling less than 600 pages, but wider recognition does seem to have quickened his pen.

The collected poems were followed in 1923 by "Roman Bartholow," a long narrative poem of a man, his wife, and a friend; and this volume was followed in 1924 by "The Man Who Died Twice," a narrative study in religious experience which brought its author for a second time the Pulitzer prize. And in 1925 appeared "Dionysus in Doubt," a collection of shorter poems which contain some fine sonnets and in which Mr. Robinson, possibly feeling nearer to a large audience than hitherto, publishes two poems dealing with modern tendencies in our life: "Dionysus in Doubt" and "Demos and Dionysus." It would be unfair to say, as I heard one critic say, that these poems were written

13

in criticism of the Eighteenth Amendment to our Constitution. Rather they are criticisms of the whole spirit of the machine age and of the idea that virtue can be legislated into people. Whether such a subject makes, not good poetry, but good poetry of the quality which Mr. Robinson habitually writes, is a question. At least the necessary formalism and the necessary confining of a very complicated issue to the two extremes of Demos, intoxicated by scientific management, versus Dionysus, make for a certain remoteness from actuality in the treatment. And the style of the poems is more suited to Mr. Robinson's other and subtler preoccupations, interests which are not the stuff of controversy.

In most of Mr. Robinson's poetry his complex and subtle style is appropriately used for studies of complex and recondite human situations. This explains, of course the slow growth of his popularity, the legend of his obscurity (which charge finds him frankly puzzled) and the rather grudging praise of English critics, especially those among them who are themselves poets in a more romantic vein.

It is true that he is a grave poet; and I remember with what unanimous choice the critics of his book, "The Man Against the Sky," seized upon and quoted a picturesque touch in "The Gift of God," a mother's crowded and enraptured vision of her son's future:

> As upward through her dream he fares,
> Half clouded with a crimson fall
> Of roses thrown on marble stairs.

First Impressions

That seemed to the critics a romantically decorative note for this austere New England poet of character and of characters and of philosophical questionings.

And yet out of that particular lion had always come sweetness. My own introduction to his work was through Floyd Dell's enthusiasm—this was many years ago—for his "The White Lights, (Broadway, 1906)," published in "The Town Down the River":

> When in from Delos came the gold
>   That held the dream of Pericles,
> When first Athenian ears were told
>   The tumult of Euripides,
> When men met Aristophanes,
>   Who fledged them with immortal quills—
> Here, where the time knew none of these,
>   There were some islands and some hills.
>
> When Rome went ravening to see
>   The sons of mothers end their days,
> When Flaccus bid Leuconoë
>   To banish her Chaldean ways,
> When first the pearled, alembic phrase
>   Of Maro into music ran—
> Here there was neither blame nor praise
>   For Rome, or for the Mantuan.
>
> When Avon, like a faery floor,
>   Lay freighted to the eyes of One,
> With galleons laden long before
>   By moonlit wharves in Avalon—

First Impressions

Here, where the white lights have begun
To seethe a way for something fair,
No prophet knew, from what was done,
That there was triumph in the air.

It might be said that that lyric is as burdened—or perhaps "loaded" is freer from the wrong sort of connotation—with thought as it is with allusions, but this is no mere superadded thought—it is lyrical thought, the actual reverberations of Broadway upon a mind that not only is associative, but also sees things in their movements, their contrasts, their perspectives. Occasionally, it is true, the poet's thought is not lyrical but purely philosophic, and then one feels that the verse form is an encumbrance. Take "Octaves," for instance, one of the poems dating from the volume, "Captain Craig." There are twenty-three octaves, and the poem is starred with fine things; but parts of it suffer from lack of definition, and the remarks that follow and comment upon the question, "Where does a dead man go?" are reminiscent of hair splitting articles on immortality and its justification in the Hibbert Journal. And that sort of thing needs space —and prose. But after all there is very little of that in Robinson. If he does have the sort of metaphysical mind that is credited to the Scotch he has also a Scotch sense of humor and a Scotch, rather than a purely New England, sternness of moral fibre. All three of these are seen in his early long poem, "Captain Craig," the tale of a derelict and philosophic soul,

16

First Impressions

rescued by a little group of friends from death by
starvation in pious Tilbury town, which

> . . . might have made him sing by feeding him
> Till he should march again, but probably
> Such yielding would have jeopardized the rhythm;
> They found it more melodious to shout
> Right on, with unmolested adoration,
> To keep the tune as it had always been,
> To trust in God, and let the Captain starve.

When, after they had:

> . . . Laid some fuel to the spark
> Of him, and oxydized it . . .

(Robinson is curiously fond of these round-about con-
ceits of expression), their beneficiary begins to treat
them to a philosophic lecture, all but the teller of the
tale

> . . . got out
> Like brokers out of Arcady . . .

But the teller stays on, and through talk, and then
through letters, and finally in a sort of will and testament which the old derelict reads to the group, we
have a wryly humorous, philosophic, and ethical commentary upon life. It is occasionally hard reading,
although there is passage after passage that is not
only philosophic but purely poetic and crystal clear
upon first reading:

17

First Impressions

> . . . Ah, friends, friends,
> There are these things we do not like to know:
> They trouble us, they make us hesitate,
> They touch us and we try to put them off.
> We banish one another and then say
> That we are left alone: the midnight leaf
> That rattles where it hangs above the snow—
> Gaunt, fluttering, forlorn—scarcely may seem
> So cold in all its palsied loneliness
> As we, we frozen brothers, who have yet
> Profoundly and severely to find out
> That there is more of unpermitted love
> In most men's reticence than most men think.

While in sentence after sentence there are such flashes of wisdom as:

> Not as a moral pedant who drags chains
> Of his unearned ideals after him . . .

And since we have spoken already of philosophy we may turn from this early poem to a comparatively recent one in which the poet philosophizes directly—indeed, it may be his answer to the charge, ridiculed recently by him in an interview, that he is a pessimist—"The Man Against the Sky." Here the figure of a man crossing the ridge of a sunset-illuminated hill, symbolizes man's journey, a journey meaningful or meaningless as it is made in the light of faith or in negation—though by faith is not implied the sort of thing that is uncritically held to be the antithesis of agnosticism:

First Impressions

Where was he going, this man against the sky?
You know not, nor do I.
But this we know, if we know anything:
That we may laugh and fight and sing
And of our transience here make offering
To an Orient word that will not be erased,
Or, save in incommunicable gleams
Too permanent for dreams,
Be found or known.

And, failing that faith, "scientific" substitutes are useless:

No soft evangel of equality
Safe cradled in a communal repose
That huddles into death, and may at last
Be covered well with equatorial snows.

—in which the positivistic ideal of an earthly paradise goes glimmering, or mere Meredithian optimism about the race:

When infant Science makes a pleasant face
And waves again that hollow toy, the Race.

The most constant interest throughout Mr. Robinson's work, however, is personality and character—often the "character" who amuses or amazes the burghers of Tilbury Town. In sonnets, or in poems only slightly longer, he presents them directly and succinctly. There is no obscurity in these poems and no moralizing, and they are among the best things he

19

has done. Poems of the same method and brevity deal with human situations, as does this sorrowfully beautiful "Souvenir":

> A vanished house that for an hour I knew
> By some forgotten chance when I was young
> Had once a glimmering window overhung
> With honeysuckle wet with evening dew.
> Along the path tall dusky dahlias grew,
> And shadowy hydrangeas reached and swung
> Ferociously; and over me, among
> The moths and mysteries, a blurred bat flew.
> Somewhere within there were dim presences
> Of days that hovered and of years gone by.
> I waited, and between their silences
> There was an evanescent, faded noise:
> And though a child, I knew it was the voice
> Of one whose occupation was to die.

Where these shorter poems do become obscure is where Mr. Robinson has two or more dramatis personae. He not only portrays subtle shades of drama—Conrad Aiken has compared him with Henry James—but he leaves his poetry between his lines. He has said that poetry should suggest rather than state explicitly. With most poets that means the use of words whose poetic quality lies in their penumbra, in their connotations rather than their mere denotation. Words, as another critic of his work, John Drinkwater, has pointed out, Robinson is apt to use for their prose value, but a prose value intensified. He gets his penumbra not from his words but as the interesting part of a situation. The actual situation he leaves for your inference from what he gives you. Poems so written gain enormously by being freed of all the prose of stage direction, of backgrounds, so to speak. They gain, that is, for the reader who finds the clue, but one sometimes has to grope for it. For instance, a poem entitled "Partnership" begins:

> Yes, you have it; I can see.
> Beautiful? Dear, look at me!
> Look, and let my shame confess
> Triumph after weariness.
> Beautiful? Ah, yes . . .

In this particular instance it is fairly obvious that what is being held up is the portrait which a husband has painted of his wife. But if a careless reader missed that, the eight remaining stanzas of the poem would be a complete puzzle; and although, to the writer, the poem "The Whip" was fairly obvious, he was once told that six faculty members—or perhaps three and their three wives—of a University in the Middle West had six differing explanations as to the facts upon which that poignant tragedy *in nuce* was built. And there are in the collected works several poems which, worry as one will, remain insoluble. Probably Mr. Robinson cannot but forget occasionally that whereas he sees from his own as well as from the reader's side of the tapestry, the reader sees only

21

his own side and cannot always connect threads which appear to him disjunctively and with no apparent connection.

These are the poems, however, of a dramatist—and one who can write with splendid imaginative insight of Shakespeare, too, as his "Ben Jonson Entertains a Man from Stratford" testifies—and after considering one other part of Mr. Robinson's work I shall call attention to one of his two plays—a beautiful piece of work which has been neglected even more than has his poetry.

That other part is his adventure into Arthurian legend: the poems "Merlin" (1917) and "Lancelot" (1920). With the exception of Miss Harriet Monroe —who thinks it a sign of weakness that a poet who can sing of to-day should deliberately turn to yesterday—the consensus is pretty nearly unanimous that in these two poems Mr. Robinson is more the poet than he has ever been. . . . So far from being a fainthearted turning to the past they are suffused by that questioning of spirit that was brought about by the war, and indeed "Merlin" bears every mark of having been written while the world was again, as when it had crumbled under Arthur, in flames. But apart from that, both poems are in that eternal present tense which is always achieved by pure poetry. And it ought not to be necessary to say that these poems are emphatically not Tennysonian. Mr. Robinson's music is a severer and more tonic music than was

First Impressions

Tennyson's yard after yard of flowing silk or satin—
or whatever the exact words were that Meredith used
in describing the Idylls. And Tennyson took Malory's
tale and pinned virtues and vices on to the characters—
so that in our memories the poem breaks up into iso-
lated bits that charm us by their music or picture:

> Elaine the fair, Elaine the beautiful,
> Elaine, the lily-maid of Astolat,

or into couplets that are tossed about by ethical lec-
turers:

> His honor rooted in dishonor grew,
> And faith unfaithful kept him falsely true.

Mr. Robinson's poems, on the other hand, musical
though they are, retain their structure because in the
first place that structure is architectural and not mere
appliqué work. In order to build such a poetic structure Mr. Robinson had to do something different from
Tennyson's *tour de force*. He had to reconstruct his
characters from the ground up. Merlin, Vivian, King
Arthur, Dagonet, Lancelot, Guinevere, Gawaine, are
no longer, as with Tennyson, borrowed characters.
They are again created for us, and live in these pages,
and their world lives, too, and trembles under their
feet, as the world of each one of us has been doing.

Merlin, in the first of these poems, is of course no
mere thaumaturge, but a wise man, and Vivian's spell
is not a stolen one of his own, but the secularly work-

ing spell of woman. For her he has deserted the eternity which is thought, and entered into time, even though Vivian has tried to make time simulate eternity by her device of exile for them both in her wooded and flower-starred paradise of Broceliande, a paradise with a clanging gate that excites Merlin's wonder:

> Why forge for this elysian wilderness
> A thing so vicious with unholy noise?

—he asks his guide as it closes upon him:

There's a way out of every wilderness
For those who dare or care enough to find it,
The guide said: and they moved along together,
Down shaded ways, through open ways with hedgerows,
And into shade again more deep than ever,
But edged anon with rays of broken sunshine
In which a fountain, raining crystal music,
Made faery magic of it through green leafage,
'Til Merlin's eyes were dim with preparation
For sight now of the lady Vivian.
He saw at first a bit of living green
That might have been a part of all the green
Around the tinkling fountain where she gazed
Upon the circling pool as if her thoughts
Were not so much on Merlin—whose advance
Betrayed through his enormity of hair
The cheeks and eyes of youth—as on the fishes,
But soon she turned and found him, now alone,
And held him while her beauty and her grace

First Impressions

Made passing trash of empires, and his eyes
Told hers of what a splendid emptiness
Her tedious world had been without him in it,
Whose love and service were to be her school,
Her triumph, and her history: "This is Merlin,"
She thought; "and I shall dream of him no more."

The poem opens, however, much later in the story than this, when Merlin, at the begging of King Arthur who feels disaster impending, comes out again through that formidable gate and goes to Camelot. On his arrival we hear Gawaine and Dagonet—the fool made knight—talking about the event. Says Gawaine:

> Men tell me that his beard has vanished wholly,
> And that he shines now as the Lord's anointed,
> And wears the valiance of an ageless youth
> Crowned with a glory of eternal peace.

But:

> Dagonet, smiling strangely, shook his head:
> "I grant your valiance of a kind of youth
> To Merlin, but your crown of peace I question;
> For, though I know no more than any churl
> Who pinches any chambermaid soever
> In the King's palace, I look not to Merlin
> For peace, when out of his peculiar tomb
> He comes again to Camelot. Time swings
> A mighty scythe, and some day all your peace
> Goes down before its edge like so much clover."

25

First Impressions

—and we are led into the atmosphere of coming disaster, the gleam of the scythe on the horizon and its shaking of the air. Merlin has indeed come out of his tomb in Vivian's Broceliande:

> Where now she crowns him and herself with flowers,
> And feeds him fruits and wines and many foods
> Of many savors, and sweet ortolans . . .
> And there are players of all instruments—
> Flutes, hautboys, drums, and viols—and she sings
> To Merlin, till he trembles in her arms,
> And there forgets that any town alive
> Had ever such a name as Camelot.

—but it is not the old Merlin:

> On his face,
> Too smooth now for a wizard or a sage,
> Lay written for the King's remembering eyes,
> A pathos of a lost authority,
> Long faded, and unconscionably gone.

But Merlin's instinct has not deserted him, and he tells the king of coming peril, peril that makes any personal misfortune—for the defection of Guinevere was the cloud on Arthur's sky—seem trivial:

> For should your force be slower then than hate,
> And your regret be sharper than your sight,
> And your remorse fall heavier than your sword—
> Then say farewell to Camelot and your crown.

. . . .

26

First Impressions

Your queen is now your kingdom, and hereafter
Let no man take it from you, or you die.
Let no man take it from you for a day;
For days are long when we are far from what
We love, and mischief's other name is distance.

But that is cold comfort:

No tide that ever crashed on Lyonesse
Drove echoes inland that were lonelier
For widowed ears among the fisherfolk,
Than for the king were memories to-night,
Of old illusions that were dead forever.

And these quotations are but typical of passage after passage throughout the poem, for beauty, insight, and cutting-edge of phrase. And in other noble passages we see Merlin's discovery that such love as Vivian's cannot outwit time. It is not that Vivian's is a guilty or unworthy love. It is simply the natural expression of a woman for whom, as yet, there is not room in man's universe of discourse:

. . . In time to be
The like of her shall have another name
Than Vivian, and her laugh shall be a fire,
Not shining only to consume itself
With what it burns. She knows not yet the name
Of what she is, for now there is no name;
Some day there shall be. Time has many names
Unwritten yet, for what we say is old
Because we are so young that it seems old.

27

First Impressions

But Merlin has seen too far: and now he sees that it will not do him or anyone else any good. Woman and "the light that Galahad found" will yet save the world, but meanwhile Camelot is doomed.

In "Lancelot" we have the same situation seen from another point of view—though the events of the story are not the same—and the same prediction of salvation through Woman and the Light worked out from the story of another love—this time that of Lancelot and Guinevere. When the poem was first published the people who objected to the criticism of Mr. Robinson that he was fleeing to an ivory tower of the past, went to the other extreme and described the poem as "a poetic interpretation of the questions and issues that have agitated us during the war and since the cessation of the war." That is perhaps putting it a little too strongly and prosaically, for both "Merlin" and "Lancelot" are beautiful things in themselves, although, in addition, it is quite evident that they are poems written "in a time of the breaking of nations," to use the phrase with which Thomas Hardy entitled that lyric contrasting the passing of nations and the permanence of purely human undertakings—ploughing and love-making. But when the breaking of nations involves ourselves, when our ploughing is interrupted, when, indeed we are, like Guinevere, nearer to the dynasty than to the plough, then tragedy is in the air. And nowadays we are, or certainly we were during the war, all near enough—to say nothing of subject to—the dynasty, so that we can feel for the tragedy of Lancelot and Guinevere: Lancelot recalled from his search for the Light by Guinevere's white and gold; Guinevere holding him in the toils of time and chance because the Light is to her a phantasm, while her love is real; until by bitter experience she learns that what goes on in time must come to an end in time and be paid for; and so herself turns to eternity, and, at Almesbury, sends Lancelot from her to his tragically deferred search for the reality that is not of the dying world of Camelot. Their love story, in humbler people a private tragedy or comedy, in its course runs athwart all the permanences and bounds of the Arthurian society, involves the downfall of Camelot, and so is a national and public tragedy.

Of the poem as a whole it may be said that it is a more straightforward tale than "Merlin" with fewer purple patches—to be accurate one should say green patches, for the lyrically descriptive parts of "Merlin" that linger in one's memory were laid in that wonderful garden of Broceliande. But certainly greater heights of purely human emotion—unmixed with what might be called metaphysical emotion—are reached; the scenes between Lancelot and Guinevere and the scene in King Arthur's chamber as he awaits the burning of Guinevere are notable.

Lancelot, of course, rescues Guinevere (one supposes, though with a little doubt, that we all remember our Arthurian legends. Certainly Mr. Robinson does not ask too much of us in that regard), and brings her to Joyous Gard. It is there he realizes that every other value of his life—his loyalty to Arthur, his former friendships—are all being smashed by his turning from the other search and taking Guinevere. If he were to kill King Arthur and Gawaine, as he could, that would be one thing. But he cannot have both worlds—his world of chivalrous devotion to the Round Table and its ideals, and his devotion to Guinevere. So, when King Arthur offers her safety, he tells Guinevere that she must return to Camelot:

> The way before you is a safer way
> For you to follow than when I was in it.
> We children who forget the whips of Time
> To live within the hour are slow to see
> That all such hours are passing. They were past
> When you came here with me.

Guinevere reproaches him for his determination:

> While he gazed on the glimmering face and hair
> Of Guinevere—the glory of white and gold
> That had been his, and were, for taking of it,
> Still his, to cloud, with an insidious gleam
> Of earth, another that was not of earth,
> And so to make of him a thing of night—
> A moth between a window and a star,
> Not wholly lured by one or led by the other.
> The more he gazed upon her beauty there,

First Impressions

The longer was he living in two kingdoms,
Not owning in his heart the king of either,
And ruling not himself.   There was an end
Of hours, he told her silent face again,
In silence.   On the morning when his fury
Wrenched her from that foul fire in Camelot,
Where blood paid irretrievably the toll
Of her release, the whips of Time had fallen
Upon them both.   All this to Guinevere
He told in silence and he told in vain.

It is perhaps unfair to expect the fullest comprehension of that passage when it is taken apart from
its context, but it may be read as a summary of the
dilemma of Lancelot, and the last line is very typical
of Robinson's fine restraint and clarity of statement.
But—leaving the solution of the difficulty for the
reader's own discovery—we may devote our few remaining sentences about this poem to calling attention
to the beauty and concision of Mr. Robinson's blank
verse which, in this poem, while packed with meaning is not so cryptic as in some of his earlier work.   It
is full of beauty of phrasing, of sudden catchings in the
verbal net of gleaming emotional moments from far beneath the surface.   His settings are felicitously used
to carry on his drama.   We first find Guinevere and
Lancelot in a garden of summer:

With oak leaves flashing in a golden light
Over her face and over her golden hair.

First Impressions

And later, in Joyous Gard, Lancelot tells her:

> We cannot make one world of two, nor may we
> Count one life more than one. Could we go back
> To the old garden, we should not stay long;
> The fruit that we should find would all be fallen
> And have the taste of earth.

And these felicities are never merely decorative. The poem all holds together, and great skill is shown in the manner in which its substance is separated from the mass of Arthurian reminiscence which surrounds it. For instance, we have Arthur's fight with Modred as part of the poem, but as Arthur's passing is not a part of it and yet will inevitably be recalled by the reader, Robinson simply "places" it for us, so that our attention does not wander. Lancelot hears of the fighting, when he comes too late to help Arthur, and hears, too, that Bedivere has gone to a hermitage:

> To think and die.   There were tales, too, of a ship.

That last sentence is simply a hand laid on a string to mute it so that it may not interfere with a further melody. A technical point, perhaps, but a witness to Robinson's great artistic sensitiveness.

Yes, this is a noble poem, straightforward in structure and high in feeling, with every temptation to pseudo-romance or mere archaeology avoided. Perhaps in no other poem of Robinson's has the psychol-

32

ogist in him yielded so unobtrusively to the poet those values which are essentially poetic.

What public attention Mr. Robinson has had since the publication of his "Collected Poems" has centered wholly around those poems, and so it is only fitting that some at least be diverted to his work as a dramatist. Of his two plays, "Van Zorn" and "The Porcupine," space only permits a note on the former—a comedy of contemporary New York life. It is a study in disinterested action—in that usually futile or disastrous action popularly known as "butting in." Van Zorn, a rich man, comes to New York after an absence of some years to find the man who calls himself his best friend, Weldon Farnham, engaged to marry Villa Vannevar, whom Van Zorn has met once, and with whom he has himself fallen in love. When he arrives upon the scene—which, in the first act, is Farnham's studio, he sees two things. From the portrait of Villa Vannevar which Farnham has painted he sees that he does not know his subject at all—that though he may wish to marry her for her beauty the real Villa Vannevar is a sealed book to him,—and he sees also that George Lucas, a brilliant man who is a ne'er-do-well, is in love with Villa and that Villa is at least interested in him—as it happens an early affair between them was broken off by Villa's conventional aunt. Indeed, his second insight is deep enough for him to tell what will be the consequence

First Impressions

to Lucas if Villa does marry Farnham. For that young man has come to the end of his moral tether.

To say that Van Zorn succeeds in straightening out this situation is to say very little of the actual drama which Mr. Robinson has built upon it. One's best friend, the woman who is pledged to marry him, and a man who is contemplating suicide are not very easy chessmen to play on a board as cluttered up as destiny has made this particular board. And so Van Zorn has carefully to consider his moves. Indeed, to get from under a figure that one sees to be inadequate, he has to reveal Lucas as a more important piece than the pawn he seems, before he can make much of a move at all. To be plain, he has to save Lucas, which can only be done, by making, on the instant, a friend of him, before he can save anyone else. Not that his failure to save Lucas would have prevented, he tells Farnham afterwards, the course of events from at least separating Farnham and the woman who was beginning to see, partly through his own portrait of her, the fact that he did not half want her.

But by sheer finesse and at the same time the forthright sincerity of his bearing, Van Zorn is able to show Villa the truth about herself. The expression of that finesse is perfect and the dialogue in which it is expressed carries one on a wave of excitement that never drops. The play was once put on, in Brooklyn, I believe, but by a company which did not do it justice. And indeed, it would take actors of great intelligence,

34

and fine feeling—and absolute docility before the author's intention—to do the play at all. For while there is nothing obscure about it, it does move by fine shades of meaning, in warnings that are only half-uttered—for a stranger, as Van Zorn almost is, cannot speak to the woman who is engaged to his best friend and not have regard to the proprieties of the situation, nor can he let those conventionalities stand in the way of the future happiness of that woman, and of the man who tries to think he loves her, and of the man who does love her. Nor can he break in upon such a situation as that and not only avoid wrecking it completely but gently undo it and rebuild it, unless he is a genius—and a disinterested one. But this is what Van Zorn does. And the manner in which he does it is absolutely convincing. The play, indeed, is as fine a piece of character creation as may be found among our modern printed plays—incomparably superior to most of the plays that are staged.

Every admirer of Mr. Robinson should read it, for it reveals the poet whom one might suspect, from partial acquaintance, to be aloof and rather stern, as having a warmly human touch and a very considerable humor. For indeed, this comedy which verges so nearly upon the tragic, has in it a most delicious humor as well as a very real depth of insight into character. In life many people try to play such a rôle as Van Zorn's but they fail and even would have failed had they possessed the rare quality of selflessness. And usually dramatists have depicted only the failures in such conduct: the "Little Miss Fix Its." Mr. Robinson is probably alone among American artists in his ability, having conceived Van Zorn, to make him successful: and he has done so in a medium where all the cards are on the table for the audience's inspection. And the reader of the play, and the spectator of it when any American manager has the good taste or courage to put it on, will come to the end with a glow of appreciation of the success, for once, of goodness and truth—and it will be not a sentimental glow merely, but an honestly evoked glow of recognition of a success honestly reached.

Robert Frost

WHEN Flaubert wished that he could write a book
about nothing, he gave the critics a phrase to quarrel
about, but he probably did not mean—as some of
the younger poets and critics have practised and
preached—that he saw beauty in a mere mosaic of
words. What he undoubtedly meant was that art
which depended on its subject, which could only seek
greatness by describing something big, which could
only evoke pity by telling a "sob story," was weak art.
On the other hand, the great artist is almost independent of subject—indeed, in principle at least, he ought
like Blake to be able to see infinity in a grain of sand.

This may sound like the opening of a plea for mysticism, but the reason that art does not need a big subject in order to be great is much simpler than one
would expect—although it may incidentally involve
mysticisim. It is that art, while in one sense a creation, is in another sense a subtraction. It renders in
its medium those aspects of life which are amenable
to that medium and it renders them stripped of non-
essentials, cleared from the disguises with which
every side of life is covered by the demands of
practical and intellectual life. We do not perceive

37

things, because our perception must immediately be transformed into concepts so that the objects of our perception may be classified and "dealt with." Life taken at its face value and not so broken up, analyzed, evaluated, would be by each perceiver taken lyrically. As Croce puts it, the first man, at the first moment of his mental life, unencumbered by abstractions or reflections, would be a poet.

The most general characteristic of the poetry of Robert Frost is just this ability to dispense with sensational subject matter and yet achieve undoubtedly poetic effects by the simple ability to come close enough to daily living to get under its skin of accustomedness, brush from its aspect the artificialities of practical life—as one would brush from one's vision of a country the artificial lines of meridians and parallels—and exhibit it in its original movement. What, for instance, could have less of a subject, from the conventional points of view: profundity, importance, sublimity, and so forth, than the lyric prefixed to the longer poems which make up "North of Boston"? Here it is:

> I'm going out to clean the pasture spring;
> I'll only stop to rake the leaves away
> (And wait to watch the water clear, I may):
> I shan't be gone long.—You come too.
>
> I'm going out to fetch the little calf
> That's standing by the mother. It's so young,

First Impressions

It totters when she licks it with her tongue.
I shan't be gone long.—You come too.

And yet how beautiful that is! And it is beautiful because the poet has brought over to us with no loss during transmission not only the picture and the invitation but the tone of voice in which the invitation is given.

Technically, it is the outstanding feature of all Mr. Frost's verse that he makes it speak in human tones. He has never written a line of free verse and he has never written a line of blank verse that does not scan— if the reader knows how to scan English verse as it should be scanned and not as Latin or Greek verse should be scanned. The reason some people have thought Mr. Frost's verses very licentiate and why others have said that he writes free verse is because he subordinates his metrical pattern to the cadences of human speech. His metrical ictus is always there but it is not always emphasized, and he is never afraid to let a logical or word accent come in a weak place metrically. His verse is at the opposite pole from that of Swinburne, who gallops to an anapaestic tune in a manner which is quite alien to human speech. On the other hand: "I shan't be gone long.—You come too" is pure and unadulterated human speech which just happens to fit into the metrical scheme of the poem. Only, such a thing "just happens" so often in Mr. Frost's work that we know that it does not

just happen at all but is the work of an exceptionally sensitive and gifted poet. And indeed Mr. Frost is so sure of the natural speech-tones in his work that he says that no one who reads his verse naturally can read it wrong. But on the other hand those who read it with a preconceived notion in their minds of how a verse should scan often find it a little difficult.

Before speaking of "North of Boston," however, the book which called the attention of the public to Mr. Frost, a few words should be said about his first book, "A Boy's Will," published in America in 1915 but first issued in England some years previously ("North of Boston" was also first issued in England, though not because American publishers refused it but simply because Mr. Frost happened to be living in England at the time when he first felt moved to collect his poems). Although "A Boy's Will" is a volume of lyrics, the author has given it unity by a series of notes under each title in the table of contents which bind the lyrics loosely together as a sort of poetic interpretation of life as he mirrors it in his own individuality. And so the reader who wishes to go behind Frost the dramatic poet, behind the recorder of New England life and character, to the subjective, almost the philosophic poet, will naturally turn to this book. And although he must not expect a lyrical poet to hand him a philosophy, he will find here some light on Frost's attitude toward the world—

he will find his gravity and his withdrawal from all
that is ephemeral; and amidst poems not so characteristic of the later Frost he will find such very characteristic ones as this:

REVELATION

We make ourselves a place apart
    Behind light words that tease and flout,
But oh, the agitated heart
    Till someone really find us out.

A pity if the case require
    (Or so we say) that in the end
We speak the literal to inspire
    The understanding of a friend.

But so with all, from babes that play
    At hide-and-seek to God afar,
So all who hide too well away
    Must speak and tell us where they are.

And characteristic, too, is the very first poem in the
book, beginning:

One of my wishes is that those dark trees,
So old and firm they scarcely show the breeze,
Were not, as 'twere, the merest mask of gloom,
But stretched away unto the edge of doom.

and picturing the poet as stealing away into their
vastness, "fearless of ever finding open land." Both

of these poems have been reprinted in a volume of selections, but a little group in the first volume that is even more self-revelatory is the one including and following the "Revelation" quoted above. After "Revelation" comes "Trial by Existence" to which is appended the note or sub-title "And to know definitely what he thinks about the soul." But the literal-minded should be warned against taking this poem literally. The argument of the poem is to the effect that in paradise we do not escape from the necessity of bravery but are destined:

> To find that the utmost reward
> Of daring should be still to dare.

And that souls in paradise are constantly being sent back to some planetary embodiment to perform some task, meet some crisis, suffer some wrong; that they are told the forthcoming sorrows if they volunteer for this service, and that they do volunteer, knowing that they will have in their new embodiment no memory of their acceptance of their lot:

> 'Tis of the essence of life here,
>   Though we choose greatly, still to lack
> The lasting memory at all clear,
>   That life has for us on the rack
> Nothing but what we somehow choose;
>   Thus are we wholly stripped of pride
> In the pain that has but one close,
>   Bearing it crushed and mystified.

42

First Impressions

I say the literal-minded reader should be warned against taking this poem literally because that would be to degrade it from a fine poem of suggestive value to a piece of theosophical dogmatism. Undoubtedly the God and heaven of this poem are fictions in somewhat the sense in which the philosopher Vaihinger says that scientific concepts such as the "atom" or "force" are fictions: they are a concrete way of stating an "as if" and doubtless what Mr. Frost is doing is, so to speak, dramatising in those anthropomorphic terms a reasoned view of suffering which shall be manlier than a mere blind hatred of it unmitigated by understanding, warmer than traditional stoicism, and a recognition that suffering is always in terms of what we are, not an alien something hitting us by chance from without but somehow or other implicit in our very constitution: just as to the idealist the world is implicit in our consciousness of it.

And perhaps another type of reader or critic ought to be warned against trying his pet procedure on another of these poems: the procedure of turning the poem either into autobiography or into that more intimate form of autobiography, the material for psychoanalysis.

This poem is entitled "In Equal Sacrifice" and is "about love." The story is told of the Douglas, who was taking the heart of Robert the Bruce to the Holy Land for sepulture, when he paused, in Spain, to fight the Moors—in a Holy War—before he should proceed further. He found himself hard-pressed, and, throwing the metal-encased heart in front of him into the fray, he followed it, exclaiming, "Heart of Death"—and perished. The poet adds:

> So may another do of right,
> Give a heart to the hopeless fight,
> The more of right the more he loves;
> So may another redouble might
>
> For a few swift gleams of the angry brand,
> Scorning greatly not to demand
> In equal sacrifice with his
> The heart he bore to the Holy Land.

In a recent book, "On English Poetry," Robert Graves, a young English poet who is interested in the new psychology, seems to imply that one does not understand a poem unless one can penetrate beneath its symbolism to the "emotional conflict" in the mind of the poet which eventuated in the release—to the poet—of expressing himself through the symbolism of the poem. But would any reader or critic have the right to say, after reading that poem, and knowing that Mr. Frost incurred great hardships because he insisted on writing poetry instead of doing what his older relatives wanted him to do,—would any reader or critic have the right to say that that poem was evidently the poet's apologia for asking those he loved to share his sacrifices? I confess that to me reading or criticism exclusively in such terms is rather repug-

nant. For whether that was the genesis of the poem
or whether the story of Douglas itself suggested the
application of the legend to the thesis of the poem
really makes no difference to the reader. All that
matters to him is the poem itself. Of course the poem
reveals the poet in this way: it shows his sense of
values in the matter of love faced with sacrifice. And
that, with the other poems so far quoted, will possibly
give the reader some idea of this New England poet
who is never a facile sentimentalist, never other than
human; grave, but also never without an abiding sense
of humor—as will be shown more particularly later.

To come back meanwhile to "North of Boston" is
perhaps to come to Frost at his greatest—though his
later work shows a widening of subject and of interest.
Here are the beautiful and humorous idylls of New
England life such as "Mending Wall' with its fine beginning:

> Something there is that doesn't love a wall
> That sends the frozen ground-swell under it,
> And spills the upper boulders in the sun

—such humorous idylls as we have in "Mountain Interval," his next book, and "New Hampshire: A
Poem with Notes and Grace Notes," which is his latest
book to date. Here are also tragic tales of the souls
whose hell is the stony loneliness and drudgery of
some New England farm: and these tragedies are
always presented to us directly—never merely told

First Impressions

at second hand. Take for example "Home Burial," in which a husband sees his wife looking, as she passes a landing window, out to the plot where the husband has recently buried their child—for many of these farms have their own burial plots—and hears, upon his challenge of her, how his apparent complacency, at any rate his lack of demonstrativeness in the first tragedy of her life, has condemned him in her eyes:

". . . And it's come to this,
A man can't speak of his own child that's dead."
"You can't because you don't know how.
If you had any feelings, you that dug
With your own hand—how could you?—his little grave;
I saw you from that very window there,
Making the gravel leap and leap in air,
Leap up, like that, like that, and land so lightly
And roll back down the mound beside the hole.
I thought, Who is that man? I didn't know you.
And I crept down the stairs and up the stairs
To look again, and still your spade kept lifting.
Then you came in. I heard your rumbling voice
Out in the kitchen, and I don't know why,
But I went near to see with my own eyes.
You could sit there with the stains on your shoes
Of the fresh earth from your own baby's grave
And talk about your everyday concerns. . . ."

And the wife goes on to repeat the very words her husband had been saying—and then the sharp climax of the poem.

First Impressions

And perhaps an even greater agony is exhibited in "A Servant to Servants"—a study in the insanity that comes upon farmers' wives who are driven beyond the limits of human endurance: and here the whole story is put in the mouth of the woman who has seen insanity in another and has herself been insane and will be so again. And yet these tales will affect only the unsophisticated as "unpleasant"—as I once heard a rich and benevolent lady say of them—for the sophisticated will recognize in their unfolding all the inevitability that makes of classical tragedy a noble pleasure.

Space forbids the exhibition of the idylls which are a relief from these tragedies; the pure comedies of New England living. And we shall see Frost the humorist when we come to "New Hampshire." I own, myself, to a special affection for some of his lyrics which are of a quality all of Frost's own, lyrical but with a touch of a very tender humor or an unpretentious wisdom. Here is one from the end of "Mountain Interval":

THE SOUND OF THE TREES

I wonder about the trees.
Why do we wish to hear
Forever the noise of these
More than another noise
So close to our dwelling place?
We suffer them by the day

First Impressions

Till we lose all measure of pace,
And fixity in our joys,
And acquire a listening air.
They are that which talks of going
But never gets away;
And that talks no less for knowing,
As it grows wiser and older,
That now it means to stay.
My feet tug at the floor
And my head sways to my shoulder
Sometimes when I watch trees sway,
From the window or the door.
I shall set forth for somewhere,
I shall make the restless choice
Some day when they are in voice
And tossing so as to scare
The white clouds over them on.
I shall have less to say,
But I shall be gone.

And while Frost's poems are never merely decorative they are filled with the most penetrating observations of Nature's smaller and shyer decorative effects. Here, for instance, is a note on the color of blueberries:

It must be on charcoal they fatten their fruit.
I taste in them sometimes the flavour of soot.
And after all really they're ebony skinned:
The blue's but a mist from the breath of the wind,
A tarnish that goes at a touch of the hand,
And less than the tan with which pickers are tanned.

48

First Impressions

There has always been humor—sometimes explicit, sometimes like that blue of the blueberry, just a faint shade—in Mr. Frost's work, although a New England poetess did once accuse him of lacking humor. His masterpiece in this kind, however, is undoubtedly "New Hampshire" in his latest volume—a book published after an interval of seven years, thereby setting more prolific poets a good example. But in the "notes and grace notes"—shorter poems and lyrics which treat in detail aspects of New Hampshire mentioned in the title-poem—we have an ascending series from humor, through beautiful genre studies, to pure lyrics. The title-poem begins:

I met a lady from the South who said
(You won't believe she said it, but she said it):
"None of my family ever worked, or had
A thing to sell." I don't suppose the work
Much matters. You may work for all of me.
I've seen the time I had to work myself.
The having anything to sell is what
Is the disgrace in man or state or nation.

I met a traveler from Arkansas
Who boasted of his state as beautiful
For diamonds and apples. "Diamonds
And apples in commercial quantities?"
I asked him, on my guard. "Oh yes," he answered,
Off his. The time was evening in the Pullman.
"I see the porter's made your bed," I told him.

49

First Impressions

I met a Californian who would
Talk California—a state so blessed,
He said, in climate—none had ever died there
A natural death, and Vigilance Committees
Had had to organize to stock the graveyards
And vindicate the state's humanity.
"Just the way Steffanson runs on," I murmured,
"About the British Arctic. That's what comes
Of being in the market with a climate." . . .

It never could have happened in New Hampshire.

But Mr. Frost's horror of salesmanship is not the horror of the lady from the South. In a poem which is a "note" to this part of the title-poem he tells of Baptiste, who was a maker of axe-helves, but not a salesman of them, although of course he did sell them—for there is a distinction between salesmanship as a thing in itself and selling so that your customer may get what he wants and enable you to get what you want. Baptiste is not a salesman because he is an artist, and as an artist he has distinct affinities with Robert Frost:

He showed me that the lines of a good helve
Were native to the grain before the knife
Expressed them, and its curves were no false curves
Put on it from without.

—which, read in terms not of wood and its grain but of speech and its natural cadence, never distorted to fit a metrical scheme, gives us precisely Frost's

50

practice in verse rhythm. And this suggests Frost, too:

> Baptiste knew how to make a short job long
> For love of it, and yet not waste time either.

In "New Hampshire" will be found, too, some essays in the supernatural. The two witch poems have that grim and humorous quality which the supernatural is apt to take on when it is exploited by—or exploits—the folk mind. In "Paul's Wife" we have another sort of supernatural—a transplanted hamadryad, already dessicated when she is first discovered. But the themes of these longer poems are so varied that most of them must be left to the reader's discovery. Among the "grace notes" "A Brook in the City" exhibits what Frost himself has called the poem with windows in it: a suggestion that is not labored enough to be called allegory, but which every reader will expand into an allegory for himself. And some of the purely lyrical poems in this section are among Frost's best. In one, "To Earthward," occurs this beautiful stanza, another example of exactitude of observation translating itself directly into poetry of high emotional tension:

> I had the swirl and ache
> From sprays of honeysuckle
> That when they're gathered shake
> Dew on the knuckle.

51

First Impressions

And Frost, never a romanticist in the cheap sense of the word, is always aware of the evanescence of things, of the instability of those elements from which we pluck beauty but to which we cannot return—for only in our memory and imagination is there the possibility of permanence for any values. And even this he can voice not as a labored thought but as the symbolism implicit in what is on its face a simple affirmation of a natural fact:

NOTHING GOLD CAN STAY

Nature's first green is gold,
Her hardest hue to hold.
Her early leaf's a flower;
But only so an hour.
Then leaf subsides to leaf.
So Eden sank to grief,
So dawn goes down to day.
Nothing gold can stay.

Carl Sandburg: Formalist

IN the layman's mind there are two kinds of physician: the up-to-date specialist with his elaborate examinations, his apparatus, and his "air"; and, on the other hand, the rough-and-ready country doctor with his absence of "air," his hail-fellow-well-met attitude, his lack of up-to-date science, and his ability to cure.

Having made this nice distinction between doctors, the public is very likely to apply it to the poets. It likes to think of some poets, Robert Bridges, for instance, as scholarly, certain, using each metrical device with intention, and knowing just what they are aiming at. And in contrast to those poets it places men of whom, in its mind, Carl Sandburg is an example: rough and ready, empirical, singing in free verse because that comes most natural to them, democratic to the verge of being—to use another of this public's words,—bolshevistic; breaking down at least the decent and orderly bounds of metre and the hedges wisely placed by their poetic forbears about the sacred plot of poetry and meant to delimit its sphere from the dirtier and dustier realm of prose.

That is precisely what a fairly large section of the public thinks of Carl Sandburg. But so called thoughts based more on analogy than on observation are usually wrong, and the public is wrong in this instance. In his poetry Carl Sandburg is very occasionally the singer of such themes as "Chicago, hog-butcher of the world"—which was an early poem; more often than that he is a pure lyrist; and he is a greater formalist than nine out of ten of the poets who use the regular verse forms, the reason for this being that those poets do not need to be formalists, finding their patterns ready made. Mr. Sandburg, eschewing patterns, has to watch his form every moment.

Curiously enough one of the important factors in the success of Mr. Sandburg's verse from a technical point of view is his use of one of the most scholarly devices that has ever been applied by English poets to their medium: the device of quantitative syllable rhythm. Indeed most English poets have echoed the old opinion of the grammarians that there is no syllable quantity in English, that with us accent takes the place of the Greek and Latin quantities so that our accented and unaccented syllables correspond to their long and short. And it is true that our heavy speech accent does override our quantity—but the quantity is there nevertheless. Here is a striking instance of what I mean. Take any line from a typical poem of Lindsay, such as

> Booth led boldly with his big bass drum

and we see that accent overrides quantity. "Bass"

is a long syllable but it is treated as a short and given
an unaccented position in the line. But in Lindsay's
collected works, one poem, "Our Mother Pocahontas,"
is prefaced by a quotation from Sandburg's poem,
"The Cool Tombs," which runs as follows:

> Pocahontas' body, lovely as a poplar, sweet as a red haw
> in November or a pawpaw in May—did she wonder? does
> she remember—in the dust—in the cool tombs?

Now it is obvious that that paragraph is rhythmical
and in a manner altogether different from the manner
in which the line quoted above is rhythmical. You
can read Sandburg's line in a monotone, suppressing
every hint of a differential accentuation, and its rhythm
will remain. Why? Because it does not depend on
accent but is inherent in the syllable lengths. So
true is this that it is only by giving each syllable its
proper length that the logical reading of the poem is
revealed. For instance a careless reader would read
the phrases: "Did she wonder? does she remember"
with a shortening of the she in each case—at least such
a reader might very easily fall into that reading. But
the real reading is

> Dĭd s͞he / wondĕr?
> Doĕs s͞he / rĕm͞em͞bĕr . . .

And the whole paragraph really reads in metrical
lines of two feet each, except the second, "Sweet
as a red haw in November," which has four, and the

penultimate line, of one, "In the dust"; the last line being scanned

In the cool / tombs.

And Mr. Sandburg achieves his extraordinarily slow pace here, the pace indeed of a funeral march, by his conjunctions of long syllables, not two in one foot, making a spondee, but letting them cut across feet, making the pace even slower. "Cool tombs" is a spondaic phrase but spreading that phrase across two feet as Mr. Sandburg does gives an even slower march.

This dry discussion of technique may seem an extraordinary approach to so human and vital a poet as Carl Sandburg but it is made largely because so many people think of him as a poet analogous to our empiric medical practitioner mentioned above. And if the reader is unconvinced and remarks that probably Sandburg himself would not understand the above analysis and might not even know what spondee was the answer would be that that has nothing to do with the case. For the language used above is notional, a convenient sort of symbolism for expressing certain facts. Sandburg may not have burdened himself with this particular set of terms. But he has produced certain very beautiful rhythmic effects—and such things are not produced by accident.

Leaving then the technique let us come to the substance of his work. Some of that work is the song of big cities and their thrust: but always from a point of

,view which transcends the big city. Sandburg is a satirist but a cosmic rather than a social satirist. For instance (from his first book, "Chicago Poems"):

LIMITED

I am riding on a limited express, one of the crack trains of the nation.

Hurtling across the prairie into blue haze and dark air go fifteen all-steel coaches holding a thousand people.

(All the coaches shall be scrap and rust and all the men and women laughing in the diners and sleepers shall pass to ashes.)

I ask a man in the smoker where he is going and he answers: "Omaha."

His social satire is more likely to be directed against communities than against individuals—though there are some glorious exceptions. But here is the beginning of one piece of social satire, "The Sins of Kalamazoo" (from "Smoke and Steel"):

The sins of Kalamazoo are neither scarlet nor crimson.

The sins of Kalamazoo are a convict gray, a dishwater drab.

And the people who sin the sins of Kalamazoo are neither scarlet nor crimson.

They run to drabs and grays—and some of them sing they shall be washed whiter than snow—and some: We should worry.

And while the next stanza mentions Main Street, it is only a few lines before we have Mr. Sandburg

57

seeing a good deal beyond Main Street; for, recognising the voice of America in this city, with all its stridences and vulgarities he also sees that:

Kalamazoo kisses a hand to something far off.
Kalamazoo calls to a long horizon, to a shivering silver angel, to a creeping mystic what-is-it.
"We're here because we're here," is the song of Kalamazoo;
"We don't know where we're going, but we're on our way," are the words.
There are hound dogs of bronze on the public square, hound dogs looking far beyond the public square . . .

When Sandburg satirizes persons it is always in their official capacities. In their unofficial capacities he loves everyone, even telling us in "Chicago Poems" how he ate steak and onions with a professional dynamiter, who "told stories of his wife and children and the cause of labor and the working class"—but who never even mentioned dynamiting,—and who is remembered by the poet chiefly as a man who does love children and laughter. And one of the tragedies of life is that the official life of the man may kill the real man. Thus, Sandburg writes a poem, in "Smoke and Steel," about "The Hangman at Home" in which he wonders what the hangman's wife and children can possibly find to ask him when he comes home after the day's work—do they have to stay off some topics?—or:

First Impressions

. . . If the little
Ones say, Daddy, play horse, here's
A rope—does he answer like a joke:
I've seen enough rope for today?
Or does his face light up like a
Bonfire of joy and does he say:
It's a good and dandy world we live
In.   And if a white face moon looks
In through a window where a baby girl
Sleeps and the moon gleams mix with
Baby ears and baby hair—the hangman—
How does he act then?   It must be easy
For him.   Anything is easy for a hangman,
I guess.

Perhaps two of the most notable poems in which men as mere officials are held up to ridicule are "To a Contemporary Bunk Shooter" in "Chicago Poems" and "And So Today" dealing with the burial of the Unknown Soldier, in "Slabs of the Sunburnt West." The first poem challenges Billy Sunday's authority to interpret the life and death of Jesus, and is couched in the slangiest vernacular:

You come along . . . tearing your shirt . . . yelling
     about Jesus.
Where do you get that stuff? . . ."

Of course that offended many religious people—who did not know when they first read it that a woman

59

Ph.D. was even then planning to include it in an anthology of the world's great religious poetry. But the slang has more than one justification. In the first place it turns Billy Sunday's own kind of language back at him, and in the second place, though this applies not so much to the actual slang as to the colloquialism, it puts Mr. Sandburg's interpretation of Jesus into words which make it actual. This is necessary, for most people have obtained their idea of the expiatory death of Jesus from stained glass windows in churches, and the whole thing is more or less of a religious decoration to them. They never visualize the crucifixion as what it was, a public execution by a barbaric and cruel method—something which Sandburg forcibly brings out in his last paragraph—and in contrast to the worldly success of Billy Sunday who will never be in any danger of suffering death or even comparative poverty for his religion.

And in the other poem mentioned Sandburg makes a picture of the sights and sounds of the funeral of "the boy nobody knows the name of" and the speech-making politicians:

> Pronouncing the syllables sac-ri-fice

carry the burden of the finest piece of satire he has done.

In "Smoke and Steel" he has tried something unlike any of his other poems, a sort of tragic and colorful symphony made up of the spectacle of steel making

First Impressions

and the lives of those who literally give those lives
to its making: one might call it a sombrely decorative
tomb-painting for all the victims of the steel-maker's
holocaust. It begins with a movement of extraordinary beauty:

Smoke of the fields in spring is one,
Smoke of the leaves in autumn another.
Smoke of a steel-mill roof or a battleship funnel,
They all go up in a line with a smokestack,
Or they twist . . . in the slow twist . . . of the wind.

If the north wind comes they run to the south.
If the west wind comes they run to the east.
By this sign all smokes know each other.
Smoke of the fields in spring and leaves in autumn,
Smoke of the finished steel, chilled and blue,
By the oath of work they swear: "I know you."

.   .   .   .

A bar of steel—it is only
Smoke at the heart of it, smoke and the blood of a man.
A runner of fire ran in it, ran out, ran somewhere else,
And left—smoke and the blood of a man
And the finished steel, chilled and blue.

So fire runs in, runs out, runs somewhere else again,
And the bar of steel is a gun, a wheel, a nail, a shovel,
A rudder under the sea, a steering-gear in the sky;
And always dark in the heart and through it,
Smoke and the blood of a man.
Pittsburgh, Youngstown, Gary,—they make their steel with
    men.

61

—and then, continuing the theme of man's blood in steel, the poem ends with another nature-note: a quiet epilogue in which steel is allowed to lie and rust while the wind directs our attention to a vastly different realm of values.

Perhaps this poem represents so far the peak of Mr. Sandburg's work. Certainly it is a splendid union of his human interests and what might be called his purely artistic interests, and so it may logically lead us to the consideration of his purely lyrical poems, embodying as it does so much material that is lyrical and in Sandburg's characteristic lyrical vein. Of course he had been writing the following kinds of poetry right along, this, for example, coming in his first book:

TROTHS

Yellow dust on a bumble bee's wing,
Grey lights in a woman's asking eyes,
Red ruins in the changing sunset embers:
I take you and pile high the memories.
Death will break her claws on some I keep.

And this impulse has been constant ever since. One of the best of the lyrics appeared in "American Poetry: 1922." This is "Windflower Leaf":

This flower is repeated
Out of old winds, out of
Old times.

First Impressions

The wind repeats these, it
Must have these, over and
Over again.

Oh, windflowers so fresh,
Oh, beautiful leaves, here
Now again.

The domes over
fall to pieces
The stones under
fall to pieces.
Rain and ice
wrecks the works.

The wind keeps, the windflowers keep, the leaves last,
The wind young and strong lets these last longer than stones.

The idea, of the transient things being the only permanent things, is a repetition of the idea of the epilogue of "Smoke and Steel" and the beauty of the lyric is enhanced, given an extraordinary thrust, through the use of colloquial expressions. That poem and others like it ought to be the touchstones by which Sandburg is judged, but at the same time, those who judge him ought not to fall into the error of one critic —a well known woman poet who has never had to work for a living and who has publicly rebuked Sandburg for writing about people who are of no account and live in alleys and slums. For, says she, the fact that they are there, shows that they are unimportant

63

in the eyes of God—God whose other name is natural selection. However, when the lady said this, Sandburg's reply was already written. He is an aesthetic poet as the above and other of our quotations show, and the reader of his books will soon learn the range of his aesthetic interest—he has even written a poem on the sculpture of Brancusi. But that an aesthetic poet had to be blind to human situations and the weight of injustice in our modern world was simply a Victorian superstition, and Sandburg's anticipatory answer to this rich lady who so easily invokes the struggle for existence is here transcribed from "Cornhuskers." It is his "Testament":

"I give the undertakers permission to haul my body to the graveyard and to lay away all, the head, the feet, the hands, all: I know there is something left over they cannot put away.

"Let the nanny goats and the billy goats of the shanty people eat the clover over my grave, and if any yellow hair or any blue smoke of flowers is good enough to grow over me let the dirty-fisted children of the shanty people pick these flowers.

"I have had my chance to live with the people who have too much and the people who have too little and I chose one of the two and I have told no man why."

But I must not end with Mr. Sandburg's testament, for that would be to imply that he was dead. Rather let me end by a word or two about his two books of prose, "Rootabaga Stories" and "Rootabaga Pigeons." These are fairy tales, but so American, so congenial to our soil are the fairies that even the Ku Klux Klan might endorse them—if that were the only point at issue. And if a living author can get so much folk spirit—especially of such a complicated folk as ours—into these tales, one might be led to postulate similar authors for the folk tales of old in place of that misty communal authorship of which the literary historians speak. Indeed after reading these books, the imaginative reader will begin to picture the origin of older folk tales somewhat after this wise: the materials meet for fairy tales floating around unrecognized; a folk saying here, a bit of wisdom there; some interesting natural object or primitive building standing out—all awaiting crystallization, but never noticed by the hurrying throng of primitive people bent on their hunting or their magical rites. And then might come a quizzical, slow-spoken, grey-headed person who perhaps dressed rather carelessly and did not care with whom he talked, who was on equally easy terms with his fellow-poets—for such a man must surely have been a poet—and with corporation lawyers (or in very primitive times with headmen of tribes); who had probably one wife and three or four children of his own, and his children were perhaps always asking him to tell them a story, and he probably told them stories and used a lot of local slang in them, and between the slang he probably got in a lot of stuff he had meant to reserve for his poems, but it just naturally slipped out. Surely out of such elements as that we can imagine very fine fairy tales to have been born.

And if that conjecture be right it is easy to see that the Rootabaga stories of Carl Sandburg are real folk art, perhaps the first real fairy stories of America that the country's spirit has ever produced—fairy stories born out of their apparent secular season, but born and thriving nevertheless, like impudently waving and hoboish grass plants between decent and law-abiding paving stones. For Carl Sandburg is not only a poet but has a wife and children, consorts with all sorts of people, and has such a beautifully creative imagination that he can not only see castles in clouds but good in moving pictures.

And so out of the combination of Sandburg and the primitive folk customs of Chicago, Ill., and vicinity, we have rising new born like Venus from the foam, or smoke from an Illinois Central engine, these two books of authentic fairy tales. That is a swifter process than the old-world one of passing them from mouth to mouth for a few hundreds of years before committing them to paper—but it has its advantages. For one thing there is more of an edge on the tales. The folk got certain effects in their tales, but to get the sharpness of the following—the sharpening up of a transaction which we avoid thinking about in its real terms because the abstract terms of the railway announce-

66

ment will better hide the tragedy often implicit in going away and never coming back—to get that we must let the individual artist do the trick. Here is the transaction in question. When Gimme the Ax's father got his ticket to go to the Rootabaga country the agent asked him:

"Do you wish a ticket to go away and come back or do you wish a ticket to go away and NEVER come back?"

There are beautiful and moving characters and episodes in these books and there is also much native American shrewdness. How many women do not, for instance, keep their watches fast on exactly the same principle which Wing Tip the Spick, the little girl from the village of Cream Puffs, who was visiting them, explained to her four uncles:

"When I was a little girl growing up, before I learned all I learned since I got older, my grandfather gave me a birthday present because I was nine years old. I remember how he said to me, 'You will never be nine years old again after the birthday, so I will give you this box for a birthday present.'

"In the box was a pair of red slippers with a clock on each slipper. One of the clocks ran fast. The other clock ran slow. And he told me if I wished to be early anywhere I should go by the clock that ran fast. And if I wished to be late anywhere I should go by the clock that ran slow."

And there is a touch of gentle raillery surely in the story of the two skyscrapers who got married—and their first child was a railroad train.   That is probably a true story and if Mr. Sandburg were pressed he could doubtless tell us the name of the god-father.   The god-mothers were undoubtedly those same widows who own all the stock in railroad trains, and whose wail is lifted up for them by the directors of the companies whenever the Interstate Commerce Commission suggests a lowering of freight rates.

But I must not give the impression that satire is the prevailing note of these books, for their prevailing tenor is that of whimsy and love, especially love of children.   And while I am writing these notes about Carl Sandburg he is writing on another work in prose. It is in a field new to Mr. Sandburg but one which he is peculiarly fitted to illumine.   A critic was told the subject of the book, and not knowing whether it would be in prose or in verse, asked Mr. Sandburg if the book "was poetry."   "I hope that there will be some poetry in it," replied Carl.   The book is a life of Abraham Lincoln.

Edgar Lee Masters: Critic of Life

EDGAR LEE MASTERS is the least occasional of our American poets: he has written lyrics—and the lyric is always a poem of occasion, though not necessarily of outer occasion—but he must be read in the large to be appreciated. Matthew Arnold is credited—unjustly—with defining poetry as a criticism of life, which, taken, as it is, without his qualifications, applies as much to suicide as it does to poetry. But whether or no poetry ought to be a criticism of life, Edgar Lee Masters' poetry is that—and sometimes it is only that.

Among the tories, of course, Mr. Masters has the reputation of being a sort of literary bolshevik, and his Spoon River was hailed as something new and strange in form as well as something ugly and materialistic in substance. It was neither. So far from being a radical in form Masters may be said to be the most literary of our contemporary poets. As a lad he studied Greek in college and read Shelley: his first poetry, published obscurely and not widely read, owed much to his reading of Shelley's poetic dramas. His "Spoon River Anthology" was regarded as something new and radical in form because so few

of his readers recognized in it the form of Book VII
of the Greek Anthology, the general form, that is, and
also a few direct translations. In his later books he
has put the sharp vintages of his Middle Western
vineyards into the old but convenient wineskins of the
Browning dramatic soliloquy. His first prose work,
"Mitch Miller," was not only modeled, in a way, on
Mark Twain's "Huckleberry Finn" and "The
Adventures of Tom Sawyer" but modeled by its
characters themselves: who read those books and
tried to live them, and the epilogue to that book was
given to us in terms of the love of Keats for Fanny
Brawne. And then "The Domesday Book" used the
form of Browning's "The Ring and the Book" to tell
its very different story.

This does not mean that Masters is imitative.
Rather the literary form he chooses enables him to
get the very maximum out of his theme. And it
certainly gives a dignity to his treatment of his theme
which might otherwise be lacking. For Masters has
led a double life, one his literary and philosophic life,
giving him both background and dignity; the other
a life as a Chicago lawyer in which dignity gave way
to the fighting instinct, a life which accustomed him,
although it did not inure him, to seeing injustice done,
a life which brought out passionate resentments and
which gave him a coarse and effective vocabulary, an
urban vocabulary one might call it, with which to
criticize judges, lawyers and law-breakers. For

instance, when Mr. Masters falls foul of William
Jennings Bryan, whose career he has followed for
years and with a growing disillusion, he lets his literary
background go for the moment, nor does he impale
his man on a rapier of wit as Edwin Arlington Robinson
might do if he could ever take cognisance of such a
figure as Bryan. No, he attacks Bryan in his own
terms:

> Who are my enemies?
> > The intelligencia, as they call themselves,
> > Who flaunt the Bible wholly or in part,
> > Or try to say that Darwin's evolution
> > Honors the Deity more than Genesis.

And so on ("The Christian Statesman" in "Starved
Rock") while in an earlier poem on Bryan, "The
Cocked Hat" ("Songs and Satires"), he actually tells
how in 1897, when Masters still believed in and
worked for Bryan, Clarence Darrow, at a banquet
("I thought it was terribly raw in him"), told Bryan:

> You'd better go back to Lincoln and study
> Science, history, philosophy,
> And read Flaubert's Madam something-or-other,
> And quit this village religious stuff.

And Mr. Masters talks in the same strain to the
upholders of what he calls our "cackle culture":

> Oh you sabbatarians, methodists, and puritans;
> You bigots, devotees, and ranters;

First Impressions

You formalists, pietists, and fanatics,
Teetotalers and hydropots . . .

telling them that, do what they will, make what laws
they choose,

> Yet there are high spaces of rapture
> Which you can never touch,
> They are beyond you and hidden from you.

And so, as a general rule, we shall find that Mr.
Masters, condemned by the nature of his profession
to live with these people, seeks his own high spaces,
and speaks in his poetic as opposed to his denunciatory voice, through literary forms that have tradition and dignity and that automatically guard him
against the contagion of the mob which he rightly
despises.

And this working through an old form was uniquely
successful in the "Spoon River Anthology." That
book is so well known that one hardly need quote
from it at this day. It is an undoubtedly veridical
picture of a small town rotten because it is out of
touch with the currents of modern life. Its people
either live parasitic lives on their poorer neighbors,
escape, by fair means or foul, or else they die, the
victims of their surroundings. But the people who
regarded the story, truly told after death, by each
member of the community, as in sum a black and
sordid chronicle did not read to the end of the book,
or read none of it understandingly. For Mr. Masters

72

did see good as well as bad; where a soul, by
some inner force or by freedom from the outer influences of the place grew in beauty and health, Mr.
Masters saw as clearly as he saw the evils of the place,
and he recorded it. There is, for example, the epitaph
of Anne Rutledge:

> Out of me unworthy and unknown
> The vibrations of deathless music:
> "With malice toward none, with charity for all."
> Out of me the forgiveness of millions toward millions,
> And the beneficent face of a nation
> Shining with justice and truth.
> I am Anne Rutledge who sleep beneath these weeds,
> Beloved in life of Abraham Lincoln,
> Wedded to him, not through union,
> But through separation.
> Bloom forever, O Republic,
> From the dust of my bosom!

And there are not only some portraits beautiful in themselves but some that indicate what is, in
fact, one of Masters' own strong bents—that toward
mysticism. Here, for example, is the portrait of "The
Village Atheist":

> Ye young debaters over the doctrine
> Of the soul's immortality,
> I who lie here was the village atheist,
> Talkative, contentious, versed in the arguments
> Of the infidels.

First Impressions

But through a long sickness
Coughing myself to death
I read the *Upanishads* and the poetry of Jesus.
And they lighted a torch of hope and intuition
And desire which the Shadow,
Leading me swiftly through the caverns of darkness,
Could not extinguish.
Listen to me, ye who live in the senses
And think through the senses only:
Immortality is not a gift,
Immortality is an achievement;
And only those who strive mightily
Shall possess it.

Indeed, in a later edition of the book, published two years after its first appearance—which was in 1914—Mr. Masters has an epilogue which itself ends, not on a note of disillusion or despair but on a note of pantheistic assertion of the unending reign of infinite life and infinite law.

"Spoon River" was followed at short intervals by "Songs and Satires," "Toward the Gulf," "Starved Rock," "Domesday Book" and "The Open Sea" in verse, while in 1920 Masters published his first work of prose fiction, "Mitch Miller," which has been followed by "Skeeters Kirby," "Children of the Market Place," "Nuptial Flight" and "Mirage."

His prose works carry on the critical warfare of his poetry. In "Mitch Miller" and "Skeeters Kirby" we see American civilization of the Lincolnian type gradually fade from the vision of the two boys who were brought up in its traditions. In "Children of the Market Place" we have a fine historical study of Stephen A. Douglas and his point of view—a point of view which had much greater justification than those of us think who were brought up on the idea that Douglas was simply the politician who took the opposite side in the famous Lincoln-Douglas Debates and on the idea, too, that the Abolitionists were the prophets of a since-achieved righteousness. In "Nuptial Flight" Masters essays a less localized theme, although the story is laid in the Middle West. It is a chronicle of marriages: a pioneer marriage, the less fortunate marriage of the boy of those pioneers to a girl from the East, and the marriage of the boy and girl of that union. And its thesis is that the woman is parasitic on her mate, not always consciously parasitic on her own behalf but unconsciously parasitic on behalf of her offspring.

To return to the poetry. We find, besides the poems directly denunciatory of present day civilization in America, a number of historical portraits, the most interesting of them being, perhaps, of early American heroes and later. In "Toward the Gulf," for instance, we have a striking portrait of Thomas Paine, as seen through the eyes of a London dramatist who revered him and would fain write a play with Paine as a hero. The poem begins with the strange story of Paine's bones being dug up by an English admirer

First Impressions

and brought to that country—to its great scandal.
The would-be dramatist finds his theme so rich that
he hardly knows how to adapt it to the exigencies
of a stageable play:

> And still
> I'd have the greatest drama in the world
> If I could prove he was dishonored, hunted,
> Neglected, libeled, buried like a beast,
> His bones dug up, thrown in and out of Chancery.
> And show these horrors overtook Tom Paine
> Because he was too great, and by this showing
> Instruct the world to honor its torch-bearers
> For time to come. No? Well, that can't be done—
> I know that; but it puzzles me to think
> That Hamilton—we'll say, is so revered,
> So lauded, toasted, all his papers studied
> On tariffs and on banks, evoking ahs!
> Great genius! and so forth—and there's the Crisis
> And Common Sense which only little Shelleys
> Haunting the dusty bookshops read at all. . . .

Possibly that passage is typical of Masters in what
we may call his middle elevation: when he is being
more than destructive and yet not at his highest
pitch. The style is a little loose, the whole thing is
colloquial but ever so often carried upward into a
flash of fine poetry as in the last clause of the quotation.

And from these American portraits he proceeds to

others: that of Voltaire—for Masters' hero is always the liberator—being a particularly fine one ("Front the Ages with a Smile") ending:

So you smiled till the lines of your mouth
A crescent became with dimples for horns, so expressing
To centuries after who see you in marble: behold me,
I lived, I loved, I laughed, I toiled without ceasing
Through eighty-four years for realities—O let them pass,
Let life go by. Would you rise over death like a god?
Front the ages with a smile.

From Voltaire, Napoleon—whom Mr. Masters sees as the great democrat thwarted by Tory England—and Shakespeare, Mr. Masters goes further back and gives us a series of Biblical studies in which his satire appears and in which it is left for something nearer to pure poetry. Some of them express not so much satire as a sort of humorous recognition of the two-sideness of those episodes in the New Testament which we use on one side only—for edification. Mr. Masters asks, for example, what were the feelings of the owner of the Gadarene swine, or of the accursed fig tree? What ought to be the culminating poem in this kind was one of the first to be published, "All Life in a Life," a portrait of Jesus in most realistic terms and with the atmosphere of his day and city denoted in terms of our own day. For instance the story of the Temptation is put in these terms:

77

First Impressions

But there was a certain sinister
Fellow who came to him hearing of his renown
And said "You can be mayor of this city,
We need a man like you for mayor."

The total effect of the poem is not, perhaps, altogether happy.

In the volumes mentioned, there is, besides the groups—though they are not arranged in groups—already mentioned, a bewildering variety of poems on problematical subjects. Poetry may be, as Wordsworth says, the finer spirit of all knowledge but it is not very likely to be the essential distillate of that which is not knowledge but problem. And hence many of these poems on such subjects as heredity and the relation of mind and brain will date: they are poetic journalism rather than poetry. And scattered among them are other poems which bear the earmarks of being left over from the poet's juvenilia. But among these works "Domesday Book" stands out as an impressive achievement. It impresses by its strength rather than by beauty of workmanship, but it is strong enough to win praise, though grudging praise, from no less prejudiced a critic than Edmund Gosse—prejudiced because he is an Englishman evaluating an American's work and because he is a classicist in taste and with an ear more attuned to the rhythms of Milton than to those of the coroner and jury at a Middle Western American inquest. But, like Words-

First Impressions

worth in certain moods, Mr. Masters has not been afraid to squeeze inquest proceedings, legal phraseology and even the evidence of a coroner's physician into the form of blank verse, and we forgive the plateaus of pedestrian versifying for the occasional risings to a climax.

The story is that of Elenor Murray, born near Starved Rock, educated largely through her own efforts—her father was a druggist disappointed with his attainments in life—and, after a season of doing war work in France, found mysteriously dead almost in the shadow of Starved Rock. The poet, utilizing her inquest, sets out to show us how every move in her life and the fact of her death, had its reverberations in other lives, and would, if its influences were traced far enough, give

> . . . a census spiritual
> Taken of our America . . .

And the terms of this census are achievement and waste. Merivale, the coroner, does not hold a merely perfunctory inquest but tries through the evidence here, as he has done in other inquests, to collect not only the immediate but the ramifying evidence, so that from his inquests he will gain data toward the solution of the great question of human waste in our civilization. He is a philosopher, a man of means, who took the coroner's office indeed with this quest in view. And so, in the death of Elenor Murray he traces

79

every separate riffle, going into the implications of
the facts as well as the facts. And the book is made
up of each witness's contribution to the unraveling of
the riddle of Elenor's death, not only as physically
caused but as the final act in a life which was achievement in part—the question is in what part? and
which in part was waste—the question is in what
degree and why?

As witness after witness testifies, we not only have
a growing revelation of the complex strands of Elenor
Murray's life but pictures of the lives that she affected. And at length Elenor Murray herself becomes
a symbol of the blindness, the struggle, the complexity,
of our national life. As one witness, the man unwit-
tingly responsible for her death, says:

>   . . . This Elenor Murray
> What was she, just a woman, a little life
> Swept in the war and broken? If no more,
> She is not worth these words: She is the symbol
> Of our America, perhaps this world
> This side of India, of America
> At least she is the symbol. What was she?
> A restlessness, a hunger, and a zeal;
> A hope for goodness, and a tenderness;
> A love, a sorrow, and a venturing will;
> A dreamer foiled but dreaming still; a vision
> That followed lures that fled her, generous, loving,
> But also avid and insatiable;
> An egoism chained and starved too long

First Impressions

That breaks away and runs; a cruelty,
A wilfulness, a dealer in false weights,
And measures of herself, her duty, others,
A lust, a slick hypocrisy and a faith
Faithless and hollow. But at last I say
She taught me, saved me for myself, and turned
My steps upon the path of making self
As much as I can make myself—my thanks
To Elenor Murray.

Taking it in the mass this is as impressive a piece of work as Masters has done since "The Spoon River Anthology." Like that work, it is, if not—to use the title of a poem already referred to—"All Life in a Life" at least a great deal of life in one life. And other personages as well as Elenor Murray stand forth and live in its pages. But it must be read for its totality and not for the sensuous satisfaction of perfect heroic lines. For when Masters is building his poems he never stops to reject imperfect bricks nor does he always trim his cement. It is not that he is incompetent—for as a matter of fact he is not. Indeed no poet could be incompetent enough—to take examples from other poems—to rhyme "wakened" and "unshakened" and it hardly reads like a typographical error, or to write the word "upborned"—no, it is not incompetence, It is a desperate hurry. It is the trick of a man so anxious to make his notes on life that he cares not for the elegance of his writing.

And indeed impatience, impatience with the stupid-

81

ity, the cruelty, and the short-sightedness of those around him must have been the mood in which much of Masters' work was written. But we must not assume that that impatience has driven him into cynicism or pessimism. Behind his anger at our fumbling with life there is a real faith in life. It is not a faith that can be formulated in any way, because life, as Masters sees it, transcends good and evil— but if life transcends not only good but evil, one cannot logically be a pessimist. And Masters has written at least one poem which already dissociates his point of view from that of the pessimist. It is "Nature" at the end of "The Open Sea"; and here is part of it:

Immeasurable Arc! To which our brief existence
Is a point, if relative, not understood.
With you endowed with motion and persistence,
Contained within you, is life evil, good?
Is life not of you? Is there aught without
By which to judge this restless brotherhood
Of will and water, and to quiet doubt
That life is good? And may the scheme deny
Itself when it is all, and rules throughout,
Knows no defeat, except as forces vie
Within it, striving? But, O Nature, you
Mother of suns and systems, what can lie
As God beyond you, making you untrue
To larger truth or being? You are all!
And man who moves within you may imbrue
His hands in war, or famine on him fall
Out of your eyeless genius, yet what wrong

First Impressions

Is wrought to your creating, magical,
Renewal, scheme? What arbiter more strong
Than you are judges discord for the strife
That stirs upon our earth, wherever throng
Thoughts, forces, fires? What is evil? Life!
Even as life is struggle, whether it smite,
Or lift, as waves to waves in will are rife
With enmity. Whatever is, is right . . .

But it would be unfair to Masters to regard him
only as the poet of broad effects, of satire, of disillusionment expressed on a semi-epical scale. For at
times he is none of these but is for a moment content
to be only a poet. To show him in this aspect I could
quote the two simple but very beautiful lyrics written
to and given the names of his daughters Marcia and
Madeline when they were small children (in "Songs
and Satires") but instead here is a line or two from
an even more poetic—because, in a manner more disinterested, study of a little servant girl, "Slip Shoe
Lovey"—and what tenderness there is under the raillery:

You're the cook's understudy,
A gentle idiot body.
You are slender like a broom
Weaving up and down the room,
With your dirt hair in a twist
And your left eye in a mist.
Never thinkin', never hopin'
With your wet mouth open.
So bewildered and so busy

First Impressions

As you scrape the dirty kettles,
O Slip Shoe Lizzie
As you rattle with the pans.
There's a clatter of old metals,
O Slip Shoe Lovey,
As you clean the milk cans.
You're a greasy little dovey,
A laughing scullery daughter,
As you slop the dish water,
So abstracted and so dizzy,
O Slip Shoe Lizzie! . . .

Some of Mr. Masters' less appreciative readers hailed his entry into the novelist's field as an advance in self-knowledge as well as in achievement. But if he is often the novelist in poetry as well as in prose he is no less a poet, too. And as a matter of fact the novel is not his choice as against poetry: rather his prose books are an interlude. And there are sides of the man—his sheer humor is one—which have not yet found their full expression in his verse. He has been accused and with some show of justice of a deficiency in the faculty of self-criticism. But that faculty may simply have been unexercised as yet. Undoubtedly when in the course of time he collects his poems he will discard many of the more ephemeral and those that deal with problems—such as heredity—whose very terms and symbols are changing. But even when he does that, a respectable canon of significant poetry will remain.

84

Vachel Lindsay: Millennialist

A FIRST glance at his book or a first hearing of one of his recitals might tempt the superficial to dub Mr. Lindsay the playboy of American poetry (if you did not wish to keep that appellation for Alfred Kreymborg). But curiously enough, this western playboy is the one poet in America to-day who wishes to give his Muse a job. Lindsay has a playful fancy and he will indulge it on any subject and unblushingly print the result, even in his collected works, but his imagination (as opposed to fancy) is not playful, or if it be playful it is the playfulness of a Campbellite Christian, of a millennium-seeking soul. Fundamentally Mr. Lindsay wants us all to be good and to be good together in a nice, neighborly, tuneful spirit. He wants us first, not only to read his poems but to meet and chant them together, and then he wants us to take that same spirit into our civic life and turn Springfield or Peoria or wherever it may be into a religious meeting house, and then he would like to see the whole world regenerated along the same lines—and I very strongly suspect that he really believes that that is what we are actually going to do some day.

The autobiographical introduction to his Collected Poems throws much light on the genesis and inspiration of all of Lindsay's work. We see him as a small boy living in the city of Abraham Lincoln, with a Kentucky religious inheritance, and we see his mother as a most extraordinary woman of genius—really he ought to write a full length biography of her—a woman of profound religious sensibilities and also of great artistic sensibilities, "putting things over" as we would now say, among her more orthodox brethren, that would be impossible to anyone else. The story, for example, of one of his mother's plays:

"One of my mother's plays was 'Olympus,' with the well-known characters, from Mercury to Father Time. My uncle, Johnson Lindsay, was Neptune, since he had a wonderful, long, beautiful red beard, and was exceedingly tall and handsome besides; a Neptune of Neptunes when draped in seaweed. The Sunday school superintendent impersonated Bacchus. How they let him get into the pulpit with all those grapes on I do not know; but he laughed hard, and Peter Paul Rubens would have been proud of him. I was too young to know what the church elders said about him. My mother was a riot in those days. How she did it in the midst of that rigor I do not know. Possibly she persuaded the elders it was like a Christmas or Easter entertainment, which had by that time been accepted as primitive, Biblical and orthodox, and in no way violating the conditions of Saint Peter's platform on the day of Pentecost.

"I know my mother called her show 'Colloquy.' It takes an epic poetess to call a heathen show a 'colloquy' and have the associated elders and deacons openly approve. . . ."

First Impressions

Even Lindsay's interest in China, the subject of one or two of his finest poems, has as a background the stories which his mother and father must have brought home from their visit to that country.

Lindsay's America, then, is an America in terms of Lincoln's political vision, Campbellite preaching, journeys to various parts of the world—especially to Europe and its art galleries—and a home in which art and literature were constant interests and in which it was assumed that he would be a painter when he grew up. He did, indeed, study drawing and as the collectors of his earlier books—especially "The Village Magazine"—know, he has always done a certain amount of it.

And a country such as this, expanding and expansive, filled with visions, is naturally the breeding place of something that at its best has many names and at its worst is called credulity. This attitude is the most constant one in Lindsay's whole life and work. We find it in these collected poems; we find it in his earlier prose works. It is at its best in his evangelic ardor, at a little less than its best in his interlude as a campaigner for the anti-saloon league: at much less than its best in his attempt to civilize the movies—even becoming a sort of prolonged adolescence in his poetical tributes to individual screen dolls, and I do not know how it will turn out in his latest idea which is to reverse the calligraphic clock and recombine writing and drawing in a new hieroglyphic language.

First Impressions

What we shall expect, then, in these poems, is primarily large and roseate vision and riotous fancy which is, however, always bent to some religious end—except when it is disporting itself with children—and a lot of very uncritical hero-worship—at least it seems uncritical to me because Lindsay's heroes do not always happen to be mine.

On the whole the most characteristic and most successful of the poems are those long ones which are meant to be chanted either by the poet to an audience or by poet and audience in responsive alternation. As this work has been referred to by Lindsay himself as a sort of higher vaudeville, and as one or two of the poems contain such syllables as "boom" or "clang," the impression has gotten abroad that Lindsay is primarily a lover of noise and "jazz"—an impression which he does not need to tell the sophisticated is totally wrong. He does tell us that, and adds that where his directions call for participation by an audience a whisper is all that is required from each throat. But this manner of poetry has cost Lindsay something. Obviously poems to be chanted have to have a definite beat. And a strong beat always makes for elementary music. And whatever Lindsay's original rhythmic possibilities were, he has sacrificed some of them, I feel sure, to this dominance of the beat. Oratory, said Mill, is heard, poetry is overheard. And although Lindsay's higher vaudeville poems are seldom mere oratory—sometimes they are—they do have to be heard and so they lose those subtle rhythmic beauties which are the possibility and the ultimate achievement of English verse. For instance, when Robert Bridges in his "London Snow"—after achieving beautiful onomatopoeic effects by his marshalling of syllables, writes these lines:

The eye marveled, marveled, at the dazzling whiteness
The ear hearkened to the stillness of the solemn air.

the rhythmic beauty of the two lines is due to the use of quantity in the classic sense. You can read the lines with no beat or stress at all, and its rhythm is not only there but makes as you read it the mood of the picture. And those lines occur in a poem in which there is not the slightest monotony of pattern— every line is expressive and different from every other line. It is the rhythm of poetry when it is most itself and least like that of the older kinds of music. Lindsay returns to the more primitive rhythm of old-fashioned music in which the beat is the most characteristic mark of the rhythm:

Booth led boldly with his big bass drum—
(Are you washed in the blood of the Lamb?). . . .
Jesus came out from the courthouse door,
Stretched his hands above the passing poor.
Booth saw not, but led his queer ones there
Round and round the mighty courthouse square. . . .

First Impressions

This was not one of Lindsay's earliest poems, although it was the one, I think, which brought him his first real fame, and it might well do so. It is one of his most successful poems, and his picture of heaven as a sort of place where they do have a courthouse square—for his and every other childhood home town had one—is, poetically, as true as it is characteristic: for Lindsay not only wants Springfield features in his heaven but would have the courthouse square in Springfield a sort of heaven—a heaven of justice, anyway—as well.

Successful, too, is "The Congo: A Study of the Negro Race," in which he gives a study that is real and yet more than merely hopeful. We all remember its beginning:

Fat black bucks in a wine-barrel room,
Barrel house kings with feet unstable
Sagged and reeled and pounded on the table,
Pounded on the table,
Beat an empty barrel with the handle of a broom,
Hard as they were able,
Boom, boom, BOOM,
With a silk umbrella and the handle of a broom,
Boomlay, boomlay, boomlay, BOOM.
THEN I had religion, THEN I had a vision.
I could not turn from their revel in derision.
THEN I SAW THE CONGO, CREEPING THROUGH
    THE BLACK,
CUTTING THROUGH THE FOREST WITH A
    GOLDEN TRACK.

90

First Impressions

And from that the poem proceeds with the vision of an actual millennial reign of righteousness on a tamed and beautiful Congo.

But with the sort of delivery and rhythm I have been speaking about, it is natural that Lindsay should occasionally forget that the printed page can only give us his intentions—short of actual directions for delivery—if the syllables actually carry the rhythm and do not have it merely imposed upon them. For instance, suppose some reader has not heard him deliver his poem, "Bryan, Bryan, Bryan, Bryan." What will such a reader make of the first line, which is:

In a nation of one hundred, fine, mob-hearted, lynching, relenting, repenting millions.

Obviously, whatever metre that line has is one forced upon it in Lindsay's own rendition, and I would respectfully suggest to him that if he intends to write any more lines like that he put in caesura marks as Francis Thompson did in some of his longer lined poems, which would at least guide the reader to the number of mouthfuls he ought to make of the line— or else he might adopt the newly rediscovered rhythmical system of punctuation used by Shakespeare and others in his day and exemplified in the new Cambridge edition of Shakespeare's works.

Among the successes in this kind, must certainly be rated that humoresque, "The Santa Fe Trail," if

First Impressions

only for its immortalizing of the Rachel Jane—the bird with no other name, according to the old negro, than just that—the bird who sings on, undefeated by the horns of all the automobiles in the United States as they race through Kansas. And indeed nearly all of these higher vaudeville poems—although I would hardly like to call "General Booth" vaudeville—are successful except "The Fireman's Ball" which has for its theme a very forced marriage of ideas indeed.

But I would like to consider the poems which are not in any sense vaudeville, which are overheard rather than heard. One of these that I particularly like—partly, perhaps, because it is a single-tax poem, is "A Net to Snare the Moonlight":

> The dew, the rain, the moonlight
> All prove our Father's mind.
> The dew, the rain, the moonlight
> Descend to bless mankind.
>
> Come, let us see that all men
> Have land to catch the rain,
> Have grass to snare the spheres of dew,
> And fields spread for the grain.
>
> Yea, we would give to each poor man
> Ripe wheat and poppies red,—
> A peaceful place at evening
> With the stars just overhead:
>
> A net to snare the moonlight,
> A sod spread to the sun,

First Impressions

A place of toil by daytime,
Of dreams when toil is done.

And I have always liked, too, "The Wedding of the Rose and the Lotus," even if it was distributed to Congress on the opening day of the Panama-Pacific exposition:

> The lotus speaks of slumber:
> The rose is as a dart.
> The lotus is Nirvana,
> The rose is Mary's heart.
> The rose is deathless, restless,
> The splendor of our pain:
> The flush and fire of labor
> That builds, not all in vain. . . .
>
> The genius of the lotus
> Shall heal earth's too-much fret
> The rose, in blinding glory,
> Shall waken Asia yet.
> Hail to their loves, ye peoples!
> Behold a world-wind blows,
> That aids the ivory lotus
> To wed the red, red rose.

Perhaps from the viewpoint of prophecy that is too evidently a poem of the days before the war. And possibly "aids . . . to wed" is a little weak. But the poem as a whole does get across.

When I said that Mr. Lindsay's heroes were apt not to be my heroes I was thinking of some later

93

characters than Lincoln, and I do share his hero-worship of John P. Altgeld, once governor of Illinois, who died in 1902. Here is Lindsay's tribute to him, one of the best poems of personal tribute in the volume:

Sleep softly . . . eagle forgotten . . . under the stone.
Time has its way with you there, and the clay has its
own.

"We have buried him now," thought your foes, and in secret
rejoiced.
They made a brave show of their mourning, their hatred
unvoiced.
They had snarled at you, barked at you, foamed at you day
after day.
Now you were ended. They praised you . . . and laid
you away.

The others that mourned you in silence and terror and
truth,
The widow bereft of her crust, and the boy without youth,
The mocked and the scorned and the wounded, the lame
and the poor
That should have remembered forever, . . . remember no
more.

Where are those lovers of yours, on what name do they
call?
The lost, that in armies wept over your funeral pall?
They call on the name of a hundred high-valiant ones,
A hundred white eagles have risen, the sons of your sons,
The zeal in their wings is a zeal that your dreaming began
The valor that wore out your soul in the service of man.

First Impressions

Sleep softly . . . eagle forgotten, . . . under the stone,
Time has its way with you there and the clay has its
    own.
Sleep on, O brave-hearted, O wise man, that kindled the
    flame—
To live in mankind is far more than to live in a name,
To live in mankind, far, far more . . . than to live in a
    name.

The fact that this volume is entitled "Collected Poems" does not mean that we can yet sum Mr. Lindsay up completely. He is not only young in years but he is young in mind. To a certain type of reader, the optimistic and millennial tone of his thought will be taken as equally indicative, as is his giving rein to mere fancy, of something immature in him. But even if we grant the immaturity—the failure of his mind to be rigidly selective—we have to admit a large number of successes in his work, successes that shine out clearly in the midst of other verses that fail by technical carelessness and lack of technical scruple—in particular I think Mr. Lindsay is far too willing to invert his adjectives for the sake of his rhymes. And sometimes these successes are in the simplest poems, where the least is apparently attempted.

But that is not the whole story, for there is one poem in the volume that shows a Lindsay new to me at least. It is near the end of the book, but as the arrangement is not strictly chronological I do not know

95

when the poem was written. In "The Perfect Marriage" Lindsay has dropped all his previous manners and optimisms. Here, we feel, is a grown-up poet who is at once grave, realistic, and high-minded. It is too long to quote, but it should be read by every one who would know Lindsay when he is not in a dancing mood nor in a mood of political exaltation, but when he sees life steadily and knows it to be, in the words of Marcus Aurelius, more like a fight than a dance.

Adelaide Crapsey: Poet and Critic

It may be substantially true, as Emerson said, that:

> One accent of the Holy Ghost
> This heedless world hath never lost, . . .

but the world has grown appreciably more heedless since Emerson wrote, with relatively fewer people in it who have time to do the necessary sifting for the authentic accents. For a few years I was almost afraid that the heedless world was going to lose the precious little collection of poetry which was published after the death of Adelaide Crapsey, especially as in one large city bookstore I saw copies of the first edition of her little book, "Verse," put on a ten cent table. But now that the volume has been reissued it is to be hoped that its intrinsic worth will overcome the world's heedlessness, and that Adelaide Crapsey will take her place as one of the outstanding woman poets of the day—a place beside Emily Dickinson and Alice Meynell, surpassing the one in self-conscious technique, and linked to the other by the fact that she was critic as well as poet, but in the company of both not only because she wrote beautiful poetry but because it is the poetry not of mere imagery but of the adventure of the spirit: the more important part of Miss Crapsey's verse dealing with the greatest adventure of all: the meeting, foreknown and awaited, with inevitable death.

That Adelaide Crapsey should have been a spiritually courageous person is not surprising to those people who know her father, Dr. Algernon Crapsey, one of the illustrious heretics of his day, a man with burning convictions and a sufferer through his expression of them. His daughter Adelaide was born in 1878, and died of tuberculosis in 1914. After her graduation from Vassar she studied at the School of Archæology in Rome, and then took up teaching as a means of livelihood, and as a life work entered upon an elaborate study of English metrics—of which I shall have more to say later.

She wrote much poetry in her earlier years, but the most part being occasional, she destroyed it, and the verse she left behind her was gathered together during the last year of her life—spent at Saranac Lake in a vain struggle against tuberculosis. Much of it indeed was written during that period—the poetry of death written by one who did not, like the average poet, think of death but who saw it coming and who deliberately shaped her sheaf of poems as a memorial:

> Wouldst thou find my ashes? Look
> In the pages of my book;
> And, as these thy hand doth turn,
> Know here is my funeral urn.

First Impressions

Miss Crapsey was a pagan in the classical rather than in the popular sense of the word, and she would have her funeral urn a thing of beauty. And so around it we find a wreath of blossoms of poetry, a small flower of a new shape: Cinquains, she called them, and they may be described as little poems that do, under the law of English prosody, what the *hokkus* and similar forms do for Japan. Of course our "free verse" writers try to write actual *hokkus* and *tankas* in English, but the results are disappointing, as there is no magic for us in a mere arbitrary number of syllables. Miss Crapsey did not merely count syllables, but devised her five line poems in an iambic series, adapted to decoration, as in "Blue Hyacinth"—

> In your
> Curled petals what ghosts
> Of blue headlands and seas,
> What perfumed immortal breath sighing
> Of Greece;

—but decoration with a far-reaching suggestiveness— and equally adapted to moods, as in "Night Winds":

> The old
> Old winds that blew
> When chaos was, what do
> They tell the clattered trees that I
> Should weep?

or, like some of the smallest of William Blake's engravings, envisaging the largest spaces:

99

First Impressions

THE GRAND CANYON

By Zeus!
Shout word of this
To the eldest dead! Titans,
Gods, Heroes, come who have once more
A home!

But even in these cinquains the poet writes of her
own death:

THE WARNING

Just now,
Out of the strange
Still dusk . . . as strange, as still . . .
A white moth flew. Why am I grown
So cold?

Not only the beauty of these cinquains but the
novelty of their form, fitting in as it did with the
fashion for experimentation, gained for them a relative
popularity, and when Miss Crapsey is quoted in
anthologies the cinquains are usually chosen. But
that, perhaps, is not fair to her other work, which
ranges from an almost tempestuous joy in life, as seen
in the two first poems of her book, written in 1905
and celebrating—

Desire on first fulfillment's radiant edge,—

to a grappling with death which is prophetic in her
poem of 1909 on John Keats:

First Impressions

Meet thou the event
And terrible happening of
Thine end: for thou art come
Upon the remote, cold place
Of ultimate dissolution and
With dumb, wide look
Thou, impotent, dost feel
Impotence creeping on
Thy potent soul. Yea, now, caught in
The aghast and voiceless pain
Of death, thyself doth watch
Thyself becoming naught.

Between the days of that prophecy and the days when Miss Crapsey wrote a similar poem about herself, the record is one of lyric joy, with a gleam here and there of a delicate humor. One sees the latter—with a sidelight on her poetic tastes, perhaps—in the lines addressed, in Fiesole, to Walter Savage Landor:

Ah, Walter, where you lived I rue
These days come all too late for me;
What matter if her eyes are blue
Whose rival is Persephone?

But we must pass over the lyrics—one or two of them suggesting Walter de la Mare—and come to that poem which is perhaps Miss Crapsey's most remarkable achievement. As she had written of the death of Keats in the cemetery of Caius Cestius, so in 1914 she addressed other dead, the dead who from the Saranac

cemetery, in sight of her own room, taunted her with
her human restlessness, and whom she, in turn, taunts
with their stillness. The gesture is a magnificent one
and probably unique in literature. A living woman,
doomed, and writing a poem with this title:

TO THE DEAD IN THE GRAVEYARD UNDER-
NEATH MY WINDOW

[Written in a Moment of Exasperation]

How can you lie so still? All day I watch,
And never a blade of all the green sod moves
To show where restlessly you turn and toss,
Or fling a desperate arm or draw up knees
Stiffened and aching from their long disuse;
I watch all night, and not one ghost comes forth
To take its freedom of the midnight hour.
Oh, have you no rebellion in your bones?
The very worms must scorn you where you lie,
A pallid, mouldering, acquiescent folk,
Meek habitants of unresented graves.
Why are you there in your straight row on row,
Where I must ever see you from my bed,
That in your mere dumb presence iterate
The text so weary in my ears, "Lie still
And rest; be patient and lie still and rest."
I'll not be patient! I will not lie still!
There is a brown road runs between the pines,
And further on the purple woodlands lie,
And still beyond blue mountains lift and loom;

First Impressions

And I would walk the road and I would be
Deep in the wooded shade and I would reach
The windy mountain tops that touch the clouds.
My eyes may follow but my feet are held.
Recumbent as you others, must I too
Submit? Be mimic of your movelessness
With pillow and counterpane for stone and sod?
And if the many sayings of the wise
Teach of submission, I will not submit,
But with a spirit all unreconciled
Flash an unquenched defiance to the stars.
Better it is to walk, to run, to dance,
Better it is to laugh and leap and sing,
To know the open skies of dawn and night,
To move untrammeled down the flaming noon,
And I will clamor it through weary days
Keeping the edge of deprivation sharp,
Nor with the pliant speaking of my lips
Of resignation, sister to defeat.
I'll not be patient. I will not lie still.

And in ironic quietude who is
The despot of our days and lord of dust
Needs but, scarce heeding, wait to drop
Grim casual comment on rebellion's end;
"Yes, yes. . . . Wilful and petulant but now
As dead and quiet as the others are."
And this each body and ghost of you hath heard
That in your graves do therefore lie so still.

From such finality as that it is perhaps well to turn
to that part of Miss Crapsey's work which being

103

prosaic is not final—which may be carried on by others. Her critical work consisted, as has been said, of an ambitious attempt to elucidate the subject of English metrics, and it was not quite completed at her death: but enough was done so that the path can be followed by others. Her book is entitled "A Study in English Metrics," and it is perhaps unique among such studies in that it takes the great body of metrical knowledge, sifts from it the essentials, and builds from them. Miss Crapsey's own contribution is an analysis which shows that what we may call the prosodic complexion of English poetry—its variety and freedom—depends not only upon its metre but upon the type of vocabulary that is adapted to that metre. Her commentators have spoken as though her work were difficult of comprehension, but this is a false appearance, due to the tabulations with which its exposition is accompanied. To understand it we have merely to remember that English metre has laws of its own which are not the laws of the Latins and Greeks. In the past we have been told that English metre paralleled Greek metre with this difference; that whereas, for instance, the iambic movement in Greek was a succession of two-syllable feet in which each first syllable was short and each second syllable long, in English the corresponding metre was made when each first syllable was unaccented and each second syllable accented. And having learned this we were then taught that good poetry consisted in lines which did not obey that law but took var-

ious exceptions to it: weak stress, inverted stress, sub-
stitutions, equivalence, and what not. The result was
not only confusing, but when the free verse writers said
that all the combinations of "feet" having been used up
by preceding poets, free verse was the only way out,
their case sounded very plausible.

Now the truth about English metre is that it is based
on time, not time in the sense of each syllable having a
definite quantity as Greek syllables had, but time in
the musical sense of the word. English verse is made
by any succession of syllables which can be recited to
a beat; this beat being marked in the case of accentual
metres by an accented syllable, and in the case of
blank verse by a syllable which is "long" rather than
accented,—for the two are not synonymous,—or even
by the knowledge in the mind of the reader that the
time-beat is on a certain syllable. Thus in the line:

I do remember an apothecary

we do not accent each even-numbered syllable: to do so
would be to give a mechanical rendering and falsify
the line; but we have to know that the metrical beat
comes on those syllables, or else the line would be
prose to us.*

* Here and in a later essay, "Free Verse and its Propaganda," I
speak of verse as being based on time. But that idea may only be
a fiction, convenient until an explanation more in accord with the
facts can take its place. I am now inclined to think that such a
truer explanation dispensing with the idea of the isochronous interval, will be found in Lascelles Abercrombie's "Principles of English
Prosody" (London).

First Impressions

What Miss Crapsey has proved is that the difference between the rhythm of one English poet and another is in large part due to their differing vocabularies, predominantly monosyllabic, moderately polysyllabic, and highly polysyllabic. The reason for this is that whenever a poet uses words of more than two syllables he is using words which have each not only an accented syllable which can mark the beat but also a syllable carrying secondary accent—which may also be used to mark the beat or which may set up a new variety of music within the line. And this new factor alters all our bases for comparing the metrical side of one poet's work with that of another's. For instance "Mother Goose" used a vocabulary predominantly monosyllabic—many of her poems being wholly so. On the other hand a poet so admired for his technical dexterity as Swinburne is seen, through Miss Crapsey's tables, to work with a predominantly monosyllabic vocabulary; in "Chastelard," indeed, the percentage of monosyllables almost approaching that of "Mother Goose"—the average occurrence of polysyllables in that poem being only 1.57. Now it is obvious that Swinburne's technical problems will be much simpler than those of such poets as Milton and Francis Thompson, who use an extremely polysyllabic vocabulary, running from seven to nine per cent of words of three syllables and over (and also a large proportion of dissyllables). Between these two extremes is the medium type of vocabulary, such as was used by Pope and Tennyson.

First Impressions

We can best see how these differences of vocabulary affect verse structure by quoting Miss Crapsey direct. After certain technical considerations, she proceeds:

> Concisely given the issue is this: When the verse is in duple rhythm (rising) the occurrence of every word over two syllables in length except mid-stress trisyllables will, if the "normal" dissyllabic foot is to be kept, force the occurrence of a syllable carrying secondary word-accent in the verse-accent place: *e.g.*: "To whom | thus Mi | chael. | Death thou | hast seen." P. L. XI. 466.

And Miss Crapsey goes on to show how the occurrence or non-occurrence of secondary word accent affects other kinds of "feet."

As applied to actual poetic criticism her insight shows us how impossible it is to compare two poets who do not work in the same vocabulary. Tennyson cannot be compared, as has been attempted, with Milton:

> Milton deals with the problems that I have indicated as inherent in a vocabulary of extreme structural complexity; his greater variety of word forms impose upon him all the difficulties of their manipulation, problems of weighting, of the management of the delicate and treacherous secondary accent syllables, and with these, since it is verse in duple rhythm, the question of variant feet. These things, if present for Tennyson, are far less acutely present and with the change in the basic condition of the vocabulary, the whole weighting and balance of the line change.

107

First Impressions

And Miss Crapsey takes an even more salient example from some criticism of Professor Gilbert Murray. That scholar, writing of what English poetry may learn from the Greek, says that metrical rhythm is one thing. Swinburne, he says, can capture the sort of rhythm needed for professed imitations of the Greek, in such work as

> She is cold and her habit is lowly. . . .

After quoting the whole stanza, he says, "This has a strong clear rhythm, full of majesty and sweetness," and he goes on to compare unfavorably with it "the most admired lyrics in "Samson Agonistes":

> God of our fathers, what is man?

and

> This, this is he: softly a while
> Let us not break in upon him. . . .
> Or do my eyes misrepresent?   Can this be he,
> That heroic, that renowned
> Irresistible Samson, whom unarmed
> No strength of man or fiercest wild beast could withstand? . . .

And of this poetry Professor Murray says: "But surely it is clear that the rhythm is exceedingly obscure and utterly unlyrical in quality?"

As I have spoken already of Miss Crapsey's rare

First Impressions

humor, and as its occasional humor is perhaps the most human thing about prosodic discussion, I may quote her answer rather fully:

Professor Murray is in all these matters of the elect, "a Roman of Rome, and very well thought of in heaven"; yet may I, even with a little decorous impishness, suggest that his words concerning Milton have a familiar sound . . . "one of the poems upon which much praise has been bestowed . . . of which the diction is harsh . . . the numbers unpleasing" . . . and thus, remembering that the great Doctor himself on occasions erred, gather courage for disagreement?

Setting aside the question of Greek metres (about which I, all wofully, know nothing) and holding to the question of English metres, in English poetry after all undeviatingly the main concern, the issue raised by any such statements seems to be this: The lines quoted by Professor Murray from Swinburne are in triple rhythm and it is Swinburne's handling of this rhythm that, at any rate "as far as metre is concerned," is oftenest given the unqualified enthusiasm of which I have spoken. It leaps to the mind in instant question—am I then to suppose that Swinburne's technique in triple rhythm is held to be, in general, comparable to the Miltonic technique in duple rhythm? It is for me an effort to phrase or squarely envisage a notion so bewildering. Yet Professor Murray seems to make the comparison—and to the discomfiture of Milton. If imperturbability is for a moment wind-blown by gusty amazements, it will I hope be forgiven me. After all there is difficulty in remaining imperturbable when one whose scholarship imposes an all wistful deference is heard saying that he "can imagine" it possible that one may "even enjoy" the rhythm of the "Samson" choruses.

The beauty of Miss Crapsey's analysis is that it not only shows us the real subtlety of English forms, but also that by placing our poets in sequence, as regards vocabulary, Milton coming at the end of a sequence of writers in duple metre and Swinburne at the beginning of a sequence, it has a heuristic value, for in its light we may predict that, assuming the main stream of English poetry to flow on, and not spread out in a swamp of free verse, we can surely say that the coming development in prosody is a mastery in triple metres —or even in quadruple—of those technical problems of a polysyllabic vocabulary which Milton mastered, working in his duple rhythms.

At any rate Miss Crapsey has left behind her the broad outlines for a treatment of English prosody which promises real results, and it is especially heartening that this exact and scientific inquiry should have been made by one who was also a poet of indubitable inspiration.

Four Younger Women Poets

In a recent book dealing with native American poetic rhythms Mary Austin remarked that poetry was not a woman's game. It may be true that we have no major poets among women at the present day, but have we among men? Fortunately, poetry does not have to be major in order to be both enjoyable and important: enjoyable for many reasons and important because sincere and therefore illuminating. And of the actual poetry written in America to-day the younger women can point to as many technical triumphs as the younger men—for Frost and Robinson we may list as majors —and to an even more interesting revelation of personality.

Of course, the word "young" is used in a very relative sense. Edna St. Vincent Millay is a younger woman than Amy Lowell, but her first volume was published in 1917, while the first volume really characteristic of Amy Lowell was issued only two years earlier—although a volume of work in which Louis Untermeyer says "it is difficult to discover even the proverbial promise" was issued in 1912. But for the purposes of this article I may put Miss Lowell on the side of the elder poets, especially as her work is

111

in a category of its own, and group as the younger woman poets of importance Edna St. Vincent Millay, Genevieve Taggard, Louise Bogan, and Elinor Wylie. Obviously, I could consider others with perhaps as much justification as these, but the poets chosen, unlike some of the more "objective" of their sisters, unite in presenting a picture of the spiritual situation in America to-day of the young, sensitive, self-conscious woman—of such a woman in a civilization which has theoretically made room for her as a person but practically has not quite caught up to her—which does not understand her, and is often aghast at her actions, and often, too, callous to her sufferings.

Miss Millay's poetry began with the publication, while she was under twenty, of that remarkable poem, "Renascence" (1912), a concrete and earthy expression of what in paler forms has been dubbed "cosmic consciousness," although by now the very use of that phrase at all calls for apology. Since then she has staked out on the field of poetry wider claims than many of her more casual readers have been aware of. While her reputation rested largely on love poetry and on what might be called the poetry of mischief and light, such things as

> My candle burns at both ends,

or

> I had a little Sorrow
> Born of a little Sin, . . .

her actual work includes poetic drama as well as the lyric, a fairly large body of narrative or semi-narrative poetry, and a number of sonnets that are as high in value as any written in our day. Even in her first volume her mastery of the sonnet is evident, as we may see from "Bluebeard"—and this is one of the poems which show that even then Miss Millay could write of love, not only in its lighter phases, but in its tragic situations:

> This door you might not open, and you did;
>   So enter now, and see for what slight thing
> You are betrayed . . . Here is no treasure hid,
>   No cauldron, no clear crystal mirroring
> The sought-for truth, no heads of women slain
>   For greed like yours, no writhings of distress,
> But only what you see . . . Look yet again—
>   An empty room, cobwebbed and comfortless.
> Yet this alone out of my life I kept
>   Unto myself, lest any know me quite:
> And you did so profane me when you crept
>   Unto the threshold of this room tonight
> That I must never more behold your face.
> This now is yours.   I seek another place.

And here, from "The Ballad of the Harp Weaver," is another sonnet directly expressive of the thing we shall find again and again in the poetry of the younger women of the present day—scorn of the sort of half-love which is too often offered them by men who are unworthy of their mettle:

113

First Impressions

Oh, oh, you will be sorry for that word!
  Give back my book and take my kiss instead.
Was it my enemy or my friend I heard,
  "What a big book for such a little head!"
Come, I will show you now my newest hat,
  And you may watch me purse my mouth and prink!
Oh, I shall love you still, and all of that.
  I never again shall tell you what I think.
I shall be sweet and crafty, soft and sly;
  You will not catch me reading any more:
I shall be called a wife to pattern by;
  And some day when you knock and push the door,
Some sane day, not too bright and not too stormy,
  I shall be gone, and you may whistle for me.

And the scale of values in which this poet measures
not only men but life may be judged from the magnificent sonnet in this same volume,

Euclid alone has looked on Beauty bare.

The work of Genevieve Taggard, not only because
we have less of it, but because it does not cover so
wide a terrain as does Miss Millay's, gives us an
impression of even greater intensity. Miss Taggard
spent her early years in Hawaii, and while she has
never exploited the islands for their mere picturesque-
ness, tropical imagery has entered largely into her
work, and this aspect of it, counterpointed, as it were,
on a native bent of mind which is disciplined rather
than tropical, clean-cut, almost stoic in its insistence

upon an inner clarity, gives us a poetry at once luxuriant and disciplined, passionate and reserved, winged and yet grounded. Miss Taggard's first volume, "For Eager Lovers"—her second, a very small one, "Hawaiian Hill Top," was published in San Francisco—carries us through the stages of a woman's life from first and disillusioned love to fulfilled love and maternity, and contains also her extraordinary picture of a cooling world, entitled "Ice Age." Again we find youth faced with disillusionment:

> We alone of all creatures—the stones more than we—
> Have no end, no motion, no destiny,

and again we have, as one of the reasons for this disillusionment the inadequacy of what is so often offered to women in the name of love:

VERY YOUNG LOVE

> Wishes are birds. You have been circled round
> With them, invisible, I sent you in distress,
> Flown from my heart that long had held them bound,
> Surpassing winds in their sharp eagerness.
>
> You have not seen their dim shades on the ground;
> Nor heard them: never felt their pinions press
> Beating the air, but never making sound,
> And hanging over you in breathlessness.
>
> So, with you here, the trembling little words
> Lie down like frightened children in the dark,

115

First Impressions

Lie down and weep; and wishes winged like birds
　　Fly crowding back; with this the only mark
That I have almost told you breathless things:
　　You hear the weary folding-down of wings.

And the section of the book in which that poem occurs ends with a sort of declaration of independence from the face-values of life:

There was a time when Mother Nature made
My soul's sun and my soul's shade. . . .

But, oh, my mother tortured me,
Blowing with wind, and sighing with sea. . . .

Until I said: "I will grow my own tree
Where no natural wind will bother me!"

And I grew me a willow of my own heart's strength,
With my will for its width, and my wish for its length:

And I made me a bird of my own heart's fire,
To sing my own sun, and my own desire. . . .

But such an attitude, of course, ought only to be provisional, and after a number of poems which express frustrations or tragedy, we come to a fourth section in which joy and fulfilment are finally captured. Here is the first poem, a poem at once purely decorative in method and yet richly expressive:

First Impressions

TALKING WATER

If you will poise your forefoot in my pool,
I will not lose a ripple, Beautiful.
Crackle the fern-stems, arch aloft and stare,
See! there's no fright for you anywhere.
A leaf shall not lift, nor a shade shake
You and your shy love away from my lake.
I know the noon is ablaze for you,
This gaunt forest, a maze for you:
Kneel near this drop of water on stone,
No one comes plunging.   You are alone.
Today I am opal, tinged with blue,
My color deepens with the glassy heat,
And I listen for hoofs.   Am I timid, too?
Noon is my enemy.   Thrust in your feet!
Trample this silver, trample this sand,
I will not startle, Little One; stand
Slim as the larch, there, I'll not take
Even your shade to the naked ache
Of my lessening waters.   If you lean,
Another faun, like you, but green
Will flick his ears and curve his throat,
His shadow hoof will lift between
These pebble-spotches.   Will you float,
Mingle and drowse and touch me, Beautiful?
If you come down some blown noon to my pool,
I will be quiet, I will be cool.

Possibly the difference between the minor and the
major poet lies in the range of experience each asks

us to share with him, the minor singer making poetry, which indeed may be perfect poetry, out of what comes to him, the major singer having a winged imagination that goes out to meet the world. If that be so, Miss Taggard is already entering her majority, for her "Ice Age" is a magnificent piece of imaginative—I was about to say re-creation, but it is a re-creation of something which has not yet happened but will: the response of man to the cooling of the earth. The poem is too long for quotation, but here is one example of its vivid picturing:

> Smoke from fire and ice's smoke
> Lunge together, fight and choke,
> Plunge and throttle and fight, and all
> Blue smoke vanishes. Ashes fall.

The poetry of Louise Bogan is probably already known to many people through her appearances in the New Republic and in a number of the magazines of poetry. Her first volume, "Body of This Death," is a small one but one of concentrated poetry. As the title implies, it is the poetry of struggle against— shall we say, circumstance? Not circumstance in the gross sense of the word, but against all that stifles, diverts, and disarms life in its original intention; against the pettiness that haunts the footsteps of love, especially against the limitations, imposed and self-imposed, on women; and, at the same time a cry for something positive, for something compelling:

118

First Impressions

Notes on the tuned frame of strings
Plucked or silenced under the hand
Whimper lightly to the ear,
Delicate or involute,
Like the mockery in a shell.
Lest the brain forget the thunder
The roused heart once made it hear—
Rising as that clamor fell—
Let there sound from music's root
One note rage can understand,
A fine noise of riven things.
Build there some thick chord of wonder:
Then, for every passion's sake,
Beat upon it till it break,

the poet sings in "Sub Contra," and "Women"—women
in general—she indicts for their failure to live
flamingly and courageously:

Women have no wilderness in them,
    They are provident instead,
Content in the tight hot cell of their hearts
    To eat dusty bread. . . .

They hear in every whisper that speaks to them
    A shout and a cry.
As like as not, when they take life over their door-sills
    They should let it go by.

It will be seen that for this mood of protest and
of assertion of an austere and uncompromising scale

119

of values Miss Bogan has an appropriately austere style, both of diction and of rhythm. Rhythmically she has learned something from Edwin Arlington Robinson, and from the later Yeats, but, like Yeats especially, she has not sacrificed beauty to this austerity—her rhythms have a very individual and moving quality. And she is not afraid to deck her beauty in imagery, natural or classical, as the following lines bear witness:

STANZA

No longer burn the hands that seized
Small wreaths from branches scarcely green.
Wearily sleeps the hardy, lean
Hunger that would not be appeased.
  The eyes that opened to white day
Watch cloud that men may look upon:
Leda forgets the wings of the swan;
  Danaë has swept the gold away,

in which the last two lines are an extraordinarily effective clinching of the matter—so effective, indeed, that the poem ought not to have been adduced as an example of beauty decked in imagery, because it is really an example of incarnation rather than of ornament. Better examples of sheer decorative resourcefulness could be taken from "A Letter," in which the author describes a visit, as a convalescent, to the country, late in autumn, when:

First Impressions

The thickets not yet stark but quivering
With tiny colors, like some brush strokes in
The manner of the pointillists; small yellows
Dart shaped, little reds in different pattern,
Clicks and notches of color on threaded bushes,
A cracked and fluent heaven, and a brown earth.

And here is the description of the countryside:

This is a countryside of roofless houses,—
Taverns to rain,—doorsteps of millstones, lintels
Leaning and delicate, foundations sprung to lilacs.
Orchards where boughs like roots strike into the sky.
Here I could well devise the journey to nothing,
At night getting down from the wagon by the black barns,
The zenith a point of darkness, breaking to bits,
Showering motionless stars over the houses.
Scenes relentless—the black and white grooves of a woodcut.

There is extraordinary resourcefulness in description there, and it is matched by Miss Bogan's sheer power when she writes poetry without any resources. What, for instance, could be more free from any poetic apparatus than this "Song":

Love me because I am lost;
Love me that I am undone.
That is brave,—no man has wished it,
Not one.

Be strong, to look on my heart
As others look on my face.
Love me,—I tell you that it is a ravaged
Terrible place.

121

First Impressions

The reader may find that some of Miss Bogan's poems are recondite. This is because she has written some of her poems of inner experience in a natural symbolism instead of directly; in a sort of dream imagery. "A Tale," the first poem in the book, though this particular poem is in the third person, is written in this manner. It must be read rather for the emotional drama which the imagery symbolizes than for any explicit story with a physical locale. "Medusa" is, on the other hand, not in the least recondite or obscure; it is simply the record in very beautiful imagery of a sort of nightmare state in which we seem "held up" in time and space. And where one or two other poems may seem obscure, the reader must make allowances for what, after all, is a natural reticence in a poet who is giving us subjective poetry distilled from what is evidently intense experience, and who must not be expected to tell us always the outer occasion as well as the inner response.

Elinor Wylie has published two books so far, "Nets to Catch the Wind" and "Black Armour." Her poetry is more often decorative than that which we have been considering, but it does sound the note common to so many of these younger woman poets of the woman's voice lifted and echoing in a rather alien world:

> What has it done, this world
> With hard finger tips,
> But sweetly chiseled and curled
> Your inscrutable lips.

First Impressions

And Mrs. Wylie has an account of her own to settle with the world: the account of inherited Puritanism. After a description in beautiful sonnets of an idyllic life in the wilds:

> When the world turns completely upside down
> You say we'll emigrate to the Eastern Shore
> Aboard a river-boat from Baltimore:
> We'll live among wild peach trees, miles from town.
> You'll wear a coonskin cap, and I a gown
> Homespun, dyed butternut's dark gold color. . . .

(That last quoted line, however, is a severe test of the reader's metrical skill)—after the description of this life and its joy and irresponsibility the poet suddenly turns round upon it all:

> Down to the Puritan marrow of my bones
> There's something in this richness that I hate. . . .

And other poems in "Nets to Catch the Wind"— notably "The Eagle and the Mole" and "Sanctuary"— show that it is not only richness that Mrs. Wylie hates but enforced gregariousness and safety, with their inevitable corollaries of immobility and suffocation. In her later book, made up of beautifully decorative poetry, but meriting, all the same, its title and subtitles taken from the armorer, there is much memorable verse, nor is the book simply the reflection of one mood nor altogether subjective. A final quotation may well be of the following poem which again illustrates the

123

First Impressions

same feminine attitude which we have found so
constantly in this poetry:

> Now let no charitable hope
>   Confuse my mind with images
> Of eagle and of antelope:
>   I am in nature none of these.
>
> I was, being human, born alone:
>   I am, being woman, hard beset:
> I live by squeezing from a stone
>   The little nourishment I get.
>
> In masks outrageous and austere
>   The years go by in single file:
> But none has merited my fear,
>   And none has quite escaped my smile.

Walter de la Mare: Poet of Tishnar

WALTER DE LA MARE has been an easy subject for reviewers. They tell us that he is the poet of one mood, that he deals in "white magic"—whatever that may be—and they lay especial stress upon his child poems. Here there is a permissible variation. If the reviewer is an unmarried youth he always adds that the child rhymes are too good for children—that only older people will appreciate them. But if he is a father he tries the poems out on his own children and does not make any such absurd statement.

Of these rhymes for and about children the greater number and the best will be found in "Peacock Pie" —included in the two volume collection of Mr. de la Mare's poetry published in 1920. A number not included in that book will be found in the book of Pamela Bianco's drawings, "Flora," for which Mr. de la Mare wrote poems illustrating the drawings— thus reversing the usual order. The poems of both books which are more especially for children have been collected, together with a few new poems, in "Down-Adown-Derry," published a year ago with drawings by Dorothy Lathrop, who also illustrated Mr. de la Mare's "The Three Mulla-Mulgars." And now comes the new edition of "A Child's Day" (first

125

First Impressions

published in England in 1912), with illustrations by Winifred Bromhall.

Miss Bianco's drawings—exhibited when she was twelve years old—have inspired Mr. de la Mare—over forty and with children older than Pamela—to poetry that will appeal not only to other children Pamela's age but to their elders as well. Such stanzas as:

> Suppose and suppose, when the gentle star
> of evening
> Came crinkling into the blue
> A magical castle we saw in the air, like a
> cloud of moonlight
> As onward we flew.

—although perhaps few children would stop to envy, as another poet might, the happiness of "crinkle." Miss Bianco's drawing of a little girl entitled "Divine Delight" has moved Mr. de la Mare to the following reflection, a far from childlike one:

> Dark, dark this mind, if ever in vain it rove
> The face of man in search of hope and love;
> Or, turning inward from earth's sun and moon,
> Spin in cold solitude thought's mazed cocoon.
> Fresh hang Time's branches. Hollow in space
> out-cry
> The grave-toned trumpets of Eternity.
> World of divine delight! heart whispereth
> Though all its all lie but 'twixt birth and
> death.

First Impressions

Though it is called a collection of "fairy poems" the selection in "Down-Adown-Derry" exhibits more than one side of Mr. de la Mare's genius. "Sam's Three Wishes; or Life's Little Whirligig" is a humorous rendering of Nietzsche's Eternal Return—achieved however, by an old farmer who innocently wished that his youth might come back. On the other hand we have such a gravely beautiful poem as "The Sunken Garden":

Speak not—whisper not;
Here bloweth thyme and bergamot;
Softly on the evening hour,
Secret herbs their spices shower.
Dark-spiked rosemary and myrrh,
Lean-stalked purple lavender;
Hides within her bosom, too,
All her sorrows, bitter rue.
Breathe not—trespass not;
Of this green and darkling spot,
Latticed from the moon's beams,
Perchance a distant dreamer dreams:
Perchance upon its darkening air,
The unseen ghosts of children fare,
Faintly swinging, sway and sweep,
Like lovely sea-flowers in its deep;
While, unmoved, to watch and ward,
Amid its gloomed and daisied sward,
Stands with bowed and dewy head
That one little leaden Lad.

127

First Impressions

The rather common mistake, in this country at least, of calling Mr. de la Mare a Georgian poet may sidetrack readers who do not know his work well. His first book, "Songs of Childhood," was written in 1902, and even his best known work, "The Listeners," came out in 1912 before the label "Georgian" had been thought of. And of course he has written as much prose as he has verse: "Henry Brocken," 1904; "The Three Mulla-Mulgars," 1910, printed in America with illustrations by Dorothy Lathrop, 1919; "The Return," a novel which won the Polignac Prize in 1911 or 1912, reissued in America in 1922; while his greatest prose work, "The Memoirs of a Midget," was one of the outstanding books of 1922. He has also written a critical brochure, "Rupert Brooke and the Intellectual Imagination."

I shall return to these books later, but meanwhile merely note how unfair it is to call the author of such a list of works the poet of a single mood. He has, indeed, a special territory and it is that of Tishnar. And as this country has been inadequately mapped I must refer the reader to "The Three Mulla-Mulgars." In a footnote in that book Mr. de la Mare explains Tishnar:

Tishnar is a very ancient word in Munza, and means that which cannot be thought about in words, or told, or expressed. So all the wonderful, secret, and quiet world beyond the Mulgars' lives is Tishnar—winds and stars, too, the endless sea and the endless unknown.

128

First Impressions

In this particular book—the adventures of three mulla-mulgars, monkeys of a royal breed who are traversing the jungle to find their hereditary country, the word is used in a more restricted sense than that given above. But in its wider sense it is Mr. de la Mare's own "Arabia Deserta" which he alone has mapped. His preoccupation with it is given us in many of his most musical poems, such as "Arabia":

Far are the shades of Arabia
  Where the Princes ride at noon,
  'Mid the verdurous vales and thickets,
  Under the ghost of the moon;
And so dark is that vaulted purple
  Flowers in the forest rise
And toss into blossom 'gainst the phantom stars
  Pale in the noonday skies.

Sweet is the music of Arabia
  In my heart when out of dreams
I still in the thin, clear mirk of dawn
  Descry her gliding streams;
Hear her strange lutes on the green banks
  Ring loud with the grief and delight
Of the dim-silked, dark-haired Musicians
  In the brooding silence of night.

They haunt me—her lutes and her forests;
  No beauty on earth I see
But shadowed with that dream recalls
  Her loveliness to me:

129

First Impressions

Still eyes look coldly upon me,
　Cold voices whisper and say—
"He is crazed with the spell of far Arabia,
　They have stolen his wits away."

The beauty of that poem speaks for itself. Its actual music is new—and the Georgians have recognized the beauty of Mr. de la Mare's rhythmical effects and have occasionally tried to imitate them. But they are of a sort that is especially hard to imitate. Any reader who already possesses the two volumes of collected poems and the later collection, "The Veil," could suggest poem after poem that might be quoted here. "The Listeners" I should never think of quoting because anyone who knows anything at all about contemporary poetry knows it and knows that it is one of the best poems of its kind written in England for the last fifty years—indeed it belongs with "Kubla Khan" and "Christabel."

But here is a little poem much less known which perhaps shows that Mr. de la Mare is as far from being an imagist as one could be:

They told me Pan was dead, but I
　Oft marveled who it was that sang
Down the green valleys languidly
　Where the grey elder thickets hang.

Sometimes I thought it was a bird
　My soul had charged with sorcery;

First Impressions

Sometimes it seemed my own heart heard
Inland the sorrow of the sea.

But even where the primrose sets
The seal of its pale loveliness,
I found amid the violets
Tears of an antique bitterness.

Ask any poet what he would give to achieve such a last line as that, and if he be a real poet he will answer you, five years of his life.

I have already in quoting "They Told Me" passed from the mood of Arabia into a more open air mood, and as so much has been made of Mr. de la Mare's adventures on the psychic borderland I am anxious to call attention to achievement of a different order. He is not only an emotional writer but a shrewd writer, and he has attempted something unique in poetic character painting. This is no less than a series of short blank verse "Characters from Shakespeare." That was a large order. We know what critics do to Shakespeare's characters, and we know that it is so difficult to do that they have even called in psycho-analysis to help them. To criticize Shakespeare according to Croce's idea of criticism—which is re-creation—is more difficult still. Mr. de la Mare has not only attempted that but he has put his re-creations into poetical form: that is to say he tries to meet Shakespeare not partly on his own ground as the Crocean critic would, but wholly on it. I think

131

that these poems have not had anything like the notice
they deserve. Here is one of them—to take a well
known character:

> Umbrageous cedars murmuring symphonies
> Stooped in late twilight o'er dark Denmark's Prince:
> He sat, his eyes companioned with dream—
> Lustrous large eyes that held the world in view
> As some entrancéd child's a puppet show.
> Darkness gave birth to the all-trembling stars,
> And a far roar of long-drawn cataracts,
> Flooding immeasurable night with sound.
> He sat so still, his very thoughts took wing,
> And, highest Ariels, the stillness haunted
> With midge-like measures; but, at last, even they
> Sank 'neath the influences of his night.
> The sweet dust shed faint perfume in the gloom;
> Through all wild space the stars' bright arrows fell
> On the lone Prince—the troubled son of man—
> On Time's dark waters in unearthly trouble:
> Then, as the roar increased, and one fair tower
> Of cloud took sky and stars with majesty,
> He rose, his face a parchment of old age,
> Sorrow hath scribbled o'er and o'er and o'er.

And, for shrewdness, we have Polonius:

> There haunts in Time's bare house an active ghost
> Enamoured of his name, Polonius.
> He moves small fingers much, and all his speech
> Is like a sampler of precisest words,
> Set in the pattern of a simpleton. . . .

132

First Impressions

While the pathos of Hamlet is matched by that of Ophelia, with her last decision:

> Better the glassy horror of the stream.

This clairvoyant ability to see wholly and walk around the characters created by other men informs another prose work of Mr. de la Mare that has recently been reprinted, "Henry Brocken."

Every imaginative reader enjoys a creative work for itself and then extends the figures in it or tries to get behind them. He thinks of something the poet or dramatist might have told us but did not. In "Henry Brocken" Mr. de la Mare does just that, but not as the casual reader would. He does it with a creative imagination which meets the first author more or less on his own ground. The framework of the story is this: An imaginative boy is brought up in solitude, in an old country house. In its library he reads all the creative triumphs of English literature. And a great itch to travel comes upon him:

> But whither?
> Now it seemed clear to me after long brooding and musing that however beautiful were these regions of which I never wearied to read, and however wild and faithful and strange and lovely the people of the books, somewhere the former must remain yet, somewhere in immortality serene, dwell they whom so many had spent life dreaming and writing about.

And one day, mounting upon a horse that comes he knows not whence, this youth rides off and visits, like Tom o' Bedlam, whose lines preface the book, the regions of which he had dreamed.

The book is written in a very beautiful poetic prose —numerous prose, the grammarians would call it— and while it might be called a *tour de force,* it is an indubitably successful one.   There is for instance the youth's meeting with the physician from "Macbeth." You remember the doctor in the fifth act of the play, who hears and sees Lady Macbeth as she walks in her sleep and tries to wash away the stains of Duncan's blood.   This doctor is living eternally with his viol and his old songs.   His visitor asks him about the tragedy, and we have in his answer a hint of a new view of the matter, as if, watching again the play from "in front," we could suddenly transport ourselves to another vantage point and see otherwise hidden expressions upon the faces of the characters. The effect cannot be reproduced here—and a very real effect it is—but I may quote a few of the introductory words to it, simply to exhibit Mr. de la Mare's glowing style in this book.   This is the morning on which the wanderer, after sleeping in an old graveyard, meets the physician:

Surely some hueless poppy blossomed in the darkness of those ruins, or the soulless ashes of the dead breathe out a drowsy influence.   Never have I slept so heavily, yet perhaps never beneath so cold a tester. Sunbeams streaming between the crests of the cypress awoke me. I leapt up as if a hundred sentinels had shouted—where none kept visible watch.

An odour of a languid sweetness pervaded the air. There was no wind to stir the dew besprinkled trees. The old, scarred gravestones stood in a thick sunshine, afloat with bees. But Rosinante had preferred to survey sunshine out of shade. In lush grass I found her, the picture of age, foot crook'd and head dejected.

As it is so much better known, little need be said here of the "Memoirs of a Midget." This is Mr. de la Mare's masterpiece in prose and undoubtedly one of the permanent contributions of the twentieth century to English literature. It is the story of a woman midget, told from within. Of good family and with a soul as sensitive as one might imagine from her size and her heredity, she lives a life of intense imagination as a child, in a garden that to her is an adventurous wilderness, and in her grown up years has to face that wilder wilderness of human beings. In this book Mr. de la Mare is at once the poet of childhood and gardens and the realist who can depict with cruel accuracy the weak and the wicked.

But I have tried in the foregoing notes to call attention rather to the less known than to the better known aspects of Mr. de la Mare's genius. Of his poems many critics have spoken. It is no exaggeration to say that he stands alone among present day English poets. And it is wrong to regard him merely as a minor poet writing disconnected lyrics. His poems taken as a whole cover a high and connected terrain. His Tishnar is a country in which we may all recognize claims which we, too, have tried to stake out. It is a country of indefinable but nevertheless real mental states—a beyond that is within. And Mr. de la Mare is a philosopher with a categorical imperative for us. It is:

> Look thy last on all things lovely,
>   Every hour. Let no night
> Seal thy sense in deathly slumber
>   Till to delight
> Thou have paid thy utmost blessings;
> Since that all things thou wouldst praise
> Beauty took from those who loved them
>   In other days.

The Later Poetry of W. B. Yeats

POETS must sometimes be disappointed at the success of their own books. We can surely imagine the shade of Rupert Brooke smiling ironically at the immense sales of his "Collected Poems" to people whose only interest in him was on account of his four war sonnets, and who had never even thought of buying his poetry until after his death with its romantic, even though tragic, circumstances. And a living poet, a friend and associate of Rupert Brooke, once thanked us for saying comparatively little of his child poems, in a review, for, as he said, they threatened to use up all the attention the public could afford to give him, leaving none for the work by which, after all, he hoped to be remembered.

With Mr. Yeats the situation of Rupert Brooke is reversed. His early poetry has become one of the accepted things to read. You meet those two gilt-backed volumes of lyrical and dramatic poetry everywhere. They are a standardized Christmas present. But do all the admirers of those poems go on to Mr. Yeats's later work? They do not. It is evident that of the small percentage of our hundred million people which read poetry only a fractional percentage read poets—have regard, that is to say, not only for the momentary gleam of the lyric or sonnet that pleases them, but for the complete revelation of the poet which begins with his first poem and ends with the last posthumous fragment given to the world by his executors.

To redress the balance in this particular instance let us take Mr. Yeats's earlier work for granted and say a word about his later. The current cant phrase about him is that he has become a man of the theatre and of theory and lost his lyric gift. And it is also added, sometimes, that he is insincere. As good a critic as Middleton Murry has found in his book, "The Wild Swans at Coole," nothing to praise and much to cavil at. But for my own part I find in that book some of the most beautiful poetry that Mr. Yeats has written, although it is beauty of a more ascetic kind than the lush exuberance of his salad days.

Of the change, of course, Mr. Yeats himself warned us in "A Coat" printed in "Responsibilities" and written between 1912 and 1914:

I made my song a coat
Covered with embroideries
Out of old mythologies
From heel to throat,
But the fools caught it,
Wore it in the world's eye
As though they'd wrought it.
Song, let them take it

138

First Impressions

For there's more enterprise
In walking naked.

The warning, however, must not be taken too literally. All of Mr. Yeats's poetry is decorative, but in this later work the decoration is of a severer order, more organic, inherent in the theme rather than adherent to it. It differs from the earlier poetry, too, in this, that Mr. Yeats comes to closer quarters with his readers. He poetizes his own experiences for us, and as his experiences have given him his philosophy, we find that his poetry and his later prose—particularly that beautiful book, "Per Amica Silentiæ Lunæ"—join in a coherent whole. And when, on the rare opportunities when it is possible for Americans, we hear his conversation, we find that that, too, links up in what, in spite of impressions that Mr. Yeats is anything from a Theosophist to a charlatan, is really a very consistent and well worked-out philosophy of life.

But for the present we are only concerned with the poetry. To say, as has been said, that Mr. Yeats's lyric gift has left him is to talk foolishly. It is at least to limit lyricism to Herrick-like song writing. In this later work we have deeper thought than before, which of course we could have without lyricism, and we have closer personal touch, but we have also a new and very exciting rhythmical subtlety—and that is the final test and the *sine qua non* of original poetry. Robert Bridges has done some new things in English poetic rhythms, but Mr. Yeats is as new and perhaps more subtle. Here for instance is a rather obscure little poem from "Responsibilities," which Mr. Yeats tells us in a note was suggested to him as he looked into the sky and at the same time thought how we tend to freeze thought "into other than human life." It has a companion piece which I do not quote:

THE MAGI

Now as at all times I can see in the mind's eye,
In their stiff, painted clothes, the pale unsatisfied ones
Appear and disappear in the blue depths of the sky
With all their ancient faces like rain-beaten stones,
And all their helms of silver hovering side by side,
And all their eyes still fixed, hoping to find once more,
Being by Calvary's turbulence unsatisfied,
The uncontrollable mystery on the bestial floor.

The rhythmic movement, itself level and unruffled like the movement of the clouds, will be obvious to whosoever reads the poem naturally, not trying to jump from stress to stress. But it is a movement which is altogether out of the orthodox limits of the usual and quite artificial method of scansion by the so-called classical feet—even though for the later lines such scansion would be possible.

And what a triumph in setting a key and keeping to it is that ending. For Calvary, according to our distance from it, physical or psychical, may be anything, from a Jewish lynching bee to a decoration in stained glass. Here, to human thought as a whole, ever tending to be distant from the reality, Calvary is simply a turbulence, unsatisfying because seen merely as that, while, in that thought-packed last line, the birth is not only pictured in its essentials but with the implication of rebuke to unsatisfied human thought in the fact that it is uncontrollable—and unrepeatable in any form that human thought may waywardly desire.

But that poem, like others in "Responsibilities," represents Mr. Yeats in a metaphysical mood, and from the point of view of a writer wishing to commend his later work to people who look askance at him, I have been guilty of bad tactics in discussing it quite so soon. For after all, the one book which may be adduced to show Mr. Yeats's great sincerity and his essential simplicity is "The Wild Swans at Coole" (1918-1919).

Indeed, if there has been a book of poems published in the English language in the last ten years of which sincerity could most assuredly be predicated, it is this collection. From the simplicity of the opening lyrics to the more labyrinthine "Ego Dominus Tuus" and "The Phases of the Moon" and "Michael Robartes" which come near the end of the book, every poem here is the direct utterance of a personal emotion or a personal discovery in imaginative reason. And not a word or rhythm is second-hand. In many of the poems the gesture is of the very simplest, but it is always a gesture of the utmost distinction—nobody could have done with those simple and simply used words just what Mr. Yeats has done. It is perhaps no exaggeration to say that there are not two consecutive lines in the volume that could not be identified as his if they were met with alone.

The book as a whole is an autumn flowering—not a mellow autumn fruitage, "close bosom-friend of the maturing sun" or drowsed with the fume of poppies—not that, but a flowering in a later and more northern autumn where only small and hardy flowers blow, where the chill of winter is already in the air, but serving as yet only to brace where summer has made languid; giving to its lovers indeed the sense of a new lease of life as they recognize that they have put away much but have much still, through now more contempla-tively, to enjoy.

That is the tone of the book as a whole, and it is remarkable how even in Mr. Yeats's smallest figures that sense of things is implied. The note is struck in the first stanza of the very beautiful poem that opens the book:

> The trees are in their autumn beauty
>   The woodland paths are dry;
> Under the October twilight the water
>   Mirrors a still sky;
> Upon the brimming water among the stones
>   Are nine and fifty swans.

142

First Impressions

The nineteenth autumn has come upon me
   Since first I made my count;
I saw, before I had well finished,
   All suddenly mount
And scatter wheeling in great broken rings
   Upon their clamourous wings.

I have looked upon those brilliant creatures,
   And now my heart is sore,
All's changed since I, hearing at twilight,
   The first time on this shore,
The bell-beat of their wings above my head,
   Trod with a lighter tread.

Unwearied still, lover by lover,
   They paddle in the cold,
Companionable streams, or climb the air;
   Their hearts have not grown old;
Passion or conquest, wander where they will,
   Attend upon them still.

But now they drift upon the still water
   Mysterious, beautiful;
Among what rushes will they build,
   By what lake's edge or pool
Delight men's eyes, when I awake some day
   To find they have flown away?

But man's heart does grow old—hungry generations do tread him down, and Mr. Yeats in a later poem tells us, rather more despondently than in many of the other poems in the book, that

First Impressions

I am worn out with dreams;
A weather-worn marble triton
Among the streams. . . .

—which gives Mr. Middleton Murry a chance to tell
him that his own romanticism is to blame, as if Mr.
Yeats were not entitled to a mood of despondency now
and then.

But these figures are consistent throughout the
volume, figures such as that of

The birds, who cry aloud
Their momentary cries before it is dawn. . . .

while that very coldness of autumn or of dawn the
poet recognizes as an ideal—knowing that it does not
imply a lack of life, but simply a certain cleansing of
life from sentimentality. Witness the poem, "The
Fisherman," in which the poet contrasts the natural
aristocrat, the peasant, with the cheap politician and
witty men and clever men of the city, and ends:

. . . Before I am old
I shall have written him one
Poem maybe as cold
And passionate as the dawn.

But this book though of autumn—the poet in one
place confesses to his fifty years—is by no means of
winter. The coldness has but stimulated the essential self, even while it may have chilled some of that
self's early exuberances. In "The Collar-Bone of a

First Impressions

Hare" Yeats pays one more tribute to the land he celebrated in that early masterpiece, "The Wandering of Oisin," and his poem beginning

> I would be as ignorant as the dawn,

with his contempt for "knowledge," will undoubtedly irritate the classicists (who will misinterpret it) as the following, "The Scholars," was, with more premeditation probably, meant to do:

> Baldheads forgetful of their sins,
> Old, learned, respectable baldheads,
> Edit and annotate the lines
> That young men, tossing on their beds,
> Rhymed out in love's despair
> To flatter beauty's ignorant ear.
>
> They'll cough in the ink to the world's end;
> Wear out the carpet with their shoes
> Earning respect; have no strange friend;
> If they have sinned nobody knows.
> Lord, what would they say
> Should their Catullus walk that way?

It is that spirit which keeps Yeats both from being wintry and from being other than aristocratic. For your aristocrat is always at ease and gay. And yet he never chooses the so-called easiest way. Here is one side of Yeats's summing up of his own relation to life and to art, and its assurance is surely justified. In lines addressed "To a Young Beauty" he says:

145

First Impressions

I know what wages beauty gives,
How hard a life her servant lives;
Yet praise the winters gone;
There is no fool can call me friend,
And I may dine at journey's end
With Landor and with Donne.

The other side of the aristocratic attitude, the gaiety of its bravery, is shown in the magnificent group of poems, "Upon a Dying Lady." The lady—we are indebted to a letter printed in *The Little Review* in which these poems first appeared—was Miss Mabel Beardsley, sister of the late Aubrey Beardsley, a Roman Catholic, who died after a lingering illness, during which Yeats and other poets and artists visited her. The poems are unique in the spirit in which they meet death, even as Miss Beardsley's meeting of it must have been a unique illustration of the attitude which Mr. T. Sturge Moore has expressed in a very beautiful poem on death in which he tells us that "imagination must teach us how to die": imagination, that is to say, in the shape of that self-consciousness which refuses to abdicate as long as there is consciousness through which it can "carry on."   Here is the first of the group which will give sufficiently the tone of them all:

HER COURTESY

With the old kindness, the old distinguished grace,
She lies, her lovely piteous head amid dull red hair

First Impressions

Propped upon pillows, rouge on the pallor of her face.
She would not have us sad because she is lying there,
And when she meets our gaze her eyes are laughter-lit,
Her speech a wicked tale that we may vie with her,
Matching our broken-hearted wit against her wit,
Thinking of saints and of Petronius Arbiter.

The seven poems of this group—like the whole book indeed—did not seem to raise a critical ripple when they were published in America. Indeed one poet wrote a letter to Miss Monroe's "Poetry" complaining that a work of genius had been overlooked, and with interest one notes that a good proportion of the poems in this book, including this group, have been reprinted by Mr. Yeats in his own selection of his works. My own opinion was from the first that the seven poems referred to will rank among the great elegies of our language—even though the hypocrisy and conventionality of the average man may regard them as blasphemous.

But that again brings us to our starting point—Mr. Yeats's sincerity. He is not a materialist, and yet in this elegy he has avoided the least touch of conventional religiosity or even poetic conventionality. And there is the same sincerity in the other elegiac poems in this volume, of old friends and of some younger friends who were killed in the war.

In vivid contrast to so many of the lesser poets of the day, Mr. Yeats is not repeating his old tunes. He is sharing with us the discoveries of his maturity,

147

and he is doing so with such unconventional sincerity that only the few will recognize his work for what it is. Not only has he made sure that there is not a fool can call him friend, but there is no sentimentalist can sully the exhibition of his heart by raving over it. The autumnal coolness of his colors and his stark, stripped line, are for tastes that have left the sentimentally luscious far behind.

Lascelles Abercrombie: Poet and Critic

WHILE popular English writers are as well known in America as in England there is a lag of a few years in our recognition of English writers in what may be called the severer modes—or at least the modes that do not appeal to popular taste. The chief reason for this is purely adventitious. It is our tariff on imported books. Unless an author is almost certain to appeal to a large audience, in which case his book will be manufactured in America, the publisher can only import a small edition in sheets and sell it at a relatively high price. That means that he cannot do anything to push the book, and so the author who is not known, so to speak, to begin with, has very little chance with the American public.

Thus Lascelles Abercrombie, one of the most widely recognized poets of the present day in England, and the author of several important works of criticism is known at first hand only to those American readers who in 1908 saw his "Interludes and Poems" or in 1912 saw "Emblems of Love," both imported by Messrs. John Lane. Since then he has published a number of books in England, but, with the exception of

149

his poems in one or two volumes of "Georgian Poetry" (Putnam) none of his work has been published in America.

That Mr. Abercrombie's work did not surmount the handicap of being imported in a very small edition is in part due to its character and our taste. His books came when we in America were having a very self-conscious renaissance of interest in poetry, and we were particularly interested at the time in free verse and in that limited sort of poetry called imagism—the appeal to the visual, tactile and auditory senses.

But if (let the injustice be condoned for the sake of convenience) we were to sum up Mr. Abercrombie in a phrase, we should have to say that he is the poet of nobility: nobility in love—and nobility contrasted with ignobility—the drama of life as lived by people with ideals, sometimes imperfect ones, but ideals which line their holders against the forces of environment. These, of course, are major themes, and our critics and anthologists were not in sympathy with them. Thus in "The New Poetry," edited by Harriet Monroe and Alice Corbin Henderson, Lascelles Abercrombie is not represented.

Born in 1881, Mr. Abercrombie in years and in certain of his publishing arrangements has been associated with the so-called Georgian group of poets— he was, for example, one of the four, Brooke, W. W. Gibson and John Drinkwater being the others, who

issued "New Numbers" a quarterly periodical of
their own work which might have been running yet
if the war had not ended its publication—and the life
of Rupert Brooke. But Mr. Abercrombie is not a
Georgian poet in the "school" sense of the term. From
his thought to his language and his rhythm he is
strikingly individual.

To read his early poetry and then to read his
theoretical essays on art is to be reminded of Yeats's
dictum that in poetry a man expresses his anti-self,
that is to say, whatever in life he is not. Thus, according to Yeats, Landor's marmoreal quality in his
verse was determined by, and was the obverse of, his
fiery tempered and passionate attitude toward life;
Keats' love of palaces and luxury in his verse were a
compensation for the lack of them in his daily living;
Lady Gregory's all-forgivingness to the characters in
her comedies the obverse of her tendency in life to
pass judgments on friend and foe. I do not think
the generalization a very sound one, but it is interesting to see how in the example of Mr. Abercrombie
a man of scholarly interests, by profession a teacher,
and a most lucid exponent of aesthetic theory, goes, in
his early poetry especially, to country people, to illiter-
ate people and to people of the most violent passions,
for his themes and situations. Indeed, with few exceptions, his characters are all people of the earth—
and country earth at that—who draw their sustenance
and their culture alike from Nature. They are people

of strong passions and he likes to exhibit them in violent crises. This does not mean that Mr. Abercrombie is melodramatic; even in his most violent dramas he is exhibiting human character, and in his later work he has depended less and less on the unusual circumstance as a factor in the drama.

The two books which I have already mentioned, "Interludes and Poems" and "Emblems of Love," are at present out of print. One of the finest poems in the earlier, and characteristic of much of the author's work, is "Blind" in which an old beggar woman has brought up her blind son with one object: when they meet the father who deserted her before the child was born, the son must use the strength of his arm to strangle the man. The lad, a natural poet in feeling, though rather "simple," is constantly being drilled in his task:

> . . . "Here, my son,
> Let me make sure again of your arms' strength:
> Ay, these are proper cords; and there'll be need
> To take him firmly when we find him, child.
> Active he is and tall and beautiful
> And a wild anger in him.—See here, boy,
> My throat's his throat; take it as you will his,
> No, tighter, tighter, where's your strength?
> Ah —"
>   Son. "O mother, did I hurt you?"
>   Mother. "Simple lad,
> You weren't half cruel enough; you barely brought
> The red flames into my eyes this time at all.

First Impressions

Oh, but it's good the grip you have, and good
To feel it on me, try the pains of those
Who strangle; they will be *his* some day."

And then the mother, leaving her son at a gorse
fire she has kindled, goes off to beg for food. The
son muses by the fire, going over in his mind those
experiences of daily life which he feels keenly but lacks
words to express—relatively, that is, for his meditation
is an opportunity which his creator does not fail to
make the most of:

I like this hour the best of all the day:
The evening cool upon my skin, the dark
And stillness, like a wing's shelter bending down.
I've often thought, if I were tall enough
And reacht my hand up, I should touch the soft
Spread feathers of the resting flight of him
Who covers us with night, so near he seems
Stooping and holding shadow over us,
Roofing the air with wings. It's plain to feel
Some large thing's near, and being good to us.
But you it is, fire, who mainly make
This time my best. I love to be alone
Except for you, and have a talk with you.
What are you? There, I'm always asking that,
And never get but laughing flames for answer.
But I believe I've found you out at last.
You, fire, are the joy of things; there's naught
Would stay in its own self, if it could find
How to be fire and joy. For you're the escape

153

First Impressions

From strictness and from nature laid on stuff
That once was freedom, still remembering it
Under its show of tameness; and there is
Nothing that is not waiting for a chance
Out of duty to slip, and give way madly
To the old desire it has in it of joy,
Standing up in a flame and telling aloud
That it is fire and no more a shape.
The wonder is, when here some leaves and furze
Have found the way to burn, the whole wide land
Leap not up in a wild glee of fire,
For all the earth's a-tiptoe to join in. . . .

That is a remarkable expression of how the feeling of life and its *élan* would be to one who is blind, and it is also one way of expressing an attitude toward life and freedom that we shall find the poet expressing again and in other ways. To come back to the drama here enacted, the boy's meditation is interrupted by the appearance of a tramp who talks to him and who, it appears, has that very skill in words which the boy is seeking. While they are talking, the mother reappears, and soon begins to recognize in this battered tramp the man who in her thought of him was still active and tall and beautiful. Her old love returns, and she—made by that return oblivious of her former intention—tells the boy that here is his father, and that from now on they will be together. The lad, thinking it his mother's cunning way of signalling him, does just what she had told him to do. And the sheer tragedy is heightened by the feeling of his mother, while she is talking to her old lover that some danger impends—but she cannot, she tells him, think what it is.

It will be seen that this is a tragedy in which circumstance plays a part, and in "Deborah," a three act play published in 1913, circumstance again plays a part—an almost Hardyan part, but in his later plays Mr. Abercrombie has put ever more emphasis upon character and less on outer happenings. Before mentioning the later plays, however, we must look into "Emblems of Love," a volume of poems on the general theme of the secular growth of love, from the days when the primitive man looked upon woman as sacred because she was the mother of the tribe's increase, through the days when she became primarily an instrument of pleasure, until the perfect fulfillment of love in self-conscious individuality. Many poets, of course, have tried to elevate love into a spiritual rather than a biological or hedonistic activity, and usually they have done it by adopting the conceptual framework of Platonism. The results have often been artificial and certainly to-day are not very convincing. Mr. Abercrombie has too keen an intellect to be satisfied with a framework which is, to modern people, only a metaphor. So instead of the Platonic idea he envisages love as a possibility—an ideal but not a pre-existent and static one. Given, then, the possibility, we are only living, in the value-creating sense

155

of the term, in so far as we strive toward that possibility. And from that point of view, remembering that the power addressed is not a thing, even a Platonic thing but a "chance" so to speak to succeed, it is no longer a Platonic conceit but a literal truth to say, as Mr. Abercrombie does say in the "Hymn to Love" announcing the theme of this volume:

> We are thine, O Love, being in thee and make of thee,
> As thou, Love, were the deep thought
> And we the speech of the thought; yea, spoken are we,
> Thy fires of thought outspoken:
>
> But burn'd not through us thy imagining
> Like fierce mood in a song caught,
> We were as clamour'd words a fool may fling,
> Loose words of meaning broken. . . .

And the hymn goes on to picture the futility of life lived merely on the natural plane and not taken up and given significance by this permanent possibility, as one might call it, of significance and meaning:

> Yea, Love, we are thine, the liturgy of thee,
> Thy thought's golden and glad name.
> The mortal conscience of immortal glee,
> Love's zeal in Love's own glory.

And as Mr. Abercrombie has placed—to drop for a moment into technicalities—accent marks on his first stanza it is evident that he sees that his stanza form

156

may be misread. The second lines have four beats, "thou, Love" each carrying a beat, and "deep thought" likewise.

Of the poems which follow, possibly "Vashti" and "Judith" are at once the most dramatic and the most revealing. In the former we have Ahasuerus's conception of love as the tired king's ivory tower and Vashti's satirical reply to him from the point of view of the woman who has become conscious of herself as person and not merely as instrument of pleasure. And in "Judith" we have the woman suddenly come into consciousness of the spirit of virginity. It is after Judith has given herself to Holofernes that she may kill him and save Bethulia that the praise of her townsmen suddenly reveals to her the spiritual uselessness of her sacrifice. It is their blindness to the essential thing that she has lost—their taking it for granted, that suddenly comes to her as an astounding insult. She turns upon them and bids them cease praising her, for she has not, after all, killed Holofernes. They assure her that it was none but she—could it be said that any one or more of them had done it?—and Judith answers:

No, nor I.
That corpse was not his death. He is alive,
And will be till there is no more a world
Filled with his hidden hunger, waiting for souls
That ford the monstrous waters of the world.
Alive in you is Holofernes now,

But fed and rejoicing; I have fed your hunger.
Yea, and alive in me: my spirit hath been
Enjoyed by the lust of the world, and I am changed
Vilely by the vile thing that clutcht on me.
Like sulphurous smoke eating into silver.
Your song is all of this, this your rejoicing;
You have good right to circle me with song!
You are the world, and you have fed on me.

But the poem should be read in its entirety to see the full force of Judith's conception of what virginity is, spiritually, and her scorn of the citizens who by the manner of their acceptance of her sacrifice show her that to them her spirit, as a thing in itself, is naught.

Mr. Abercrombie's later poetry, with one or two exceptions, notably "The Sale of St. Thomas," has been in dramatic form and is included in "Four Short Plays" (London: Secker. 1922) and "Phoenix" (Secker. 1923). Of the short plays "The End of the World" may be mentioned for its humorous exploitation of the reactions of a number of people to the prospect of the imminent destruction of the world. The characters are country people, a farmer, a wainwright, a carpenter and others. An extremely hot day, with a haystack fire on the horizon gives color to the tale of a wandering "dowser"—a man who finds hidden water—that a comet then visible in the sky is about to collide with the earth and end it. What ensues may be called a comedy of the transvaluation of values. Huff, the self-righteous carpenter, to take one example, at first greets the coming event as if it had been staged expressly to punish Shale, the laborer, and Huff's wife with whom Shale had run away—though he had not even done Huff the honor of running very far—some time ago. He gloats over the picture of Shale and Mrs. Huff cringing as they begin to feel the ineluctable rise of temperature, while he, the righteous man who left even his vengeance to God remains psychically and, one would imagine from his talk, even physically cool. But when he does begin to think about himself and his past life a curious thing happens. The essentially factitious nature of his piety is revealed by his sudden repentance of it. He remembers opportunities for carnal sin that he had not taken advantage of, and as it was really fear and not goodness that had prompted this abstinence he is now regretting it. And into the midst of this regret Shale walks into the inn parlor, dragging Mrs. Huff whom he would fain deliver to her rightful lord so that he may not have her on his hands in the final moment. The whole thing is done with a fine sense of humor, a command of a true country speech that is yet raised to the level of poetry, and a real insight into human nature.

In "Phoenix: a Tragicomedy," the latest of Mr. Abercrombie's plays, we have a study of nobility, ignobility, and a simple and natural sort of non-nobility that is not ignoble. Phoenix is a young Prince in a small and ancient Grecian kingdom, and just when he

159

has killed his first tiger and is enraptured with the life of manly action, he comes home to find that his father has a strange woman in the palace. Phoenix does not know that she is a bought woman with whom the old king fancies himself in love. The queen, jealous of her rights and status, uses Phoenix to lure the bought woman from the king: and succeeds but at a cost which she had not reckoned. It is a tragicomedy in which the comedy is a subtle revelation of the ignobility of the king's character and the utter simplicity of Rhodope's. When the king brings her to the top of his palace he talks in this strain:

Amyntor. This is my pleasant place; and here we'll keep
  A kind of heaven, where we shall find our moods
  Made one with things. For look how white and smooth
  Idleness has become a marble palace;
  And this is our day-dreaming passion glowing
  Over it, this blue and shadowy night.
  O colored like the summer of the gods
  Our life shall be up here; here it shall pause
  Like that immortal fortune of the gods
  In unconcerned perfection of ourselves.
  No world's left here for love to gaze upon
  But what must seem love's imagery—the blue
  Trembling flame of the sea's infinite gleam,
  And clouded snows that pace about the air
  With towering motion, breathing shadowless light.

And the language that would be fitting as well as beautiful for two young lovers in an empty world is,

160

in its very height, the index of the depths of ignominy, coming from a senile king and addressed to a slave whom he has bought for money. Indeed the slave is herself not ignoble at all, for she is frank. She yawns at this harangue:

Ah—La!
The bench is comfortable and the view pretty.
But not all day up here, surely!—A goddess,
When she can wear the love of a wealthy god,
Needs to show off.

And Rhodope has sense enough to see, too, that a heaven with an enraged wife intruding on it and two sentries prying on what is going on is hardly worthy of the king's superlative characterizations of it as the care-free abode of perfect love.

We must be content with a very rapid survey of Mr. Abercrombie's critical work. It ranges from a philosophical, and aesthetic appreciation of the writings of Thomas Hardy to a detailed study of "The Principles of English Prosody," of which the first part only is yet published. Then, though we must mention, in passing, his philosophical work, "Speculative Dialogues," we have a short study of "The Epic" and, most important of all perhaps, his two latest books in this kind, "Towards a Theory of Art" and "The Theory of Poetry," in which the principles of the more general work are applied to poetry in particular. "Towards a Theory of Art" is the only work which I will consider here. Mr. Abercrombie starts out in agreement with Croce that a work of art is a technique which enables the spectator to reproduce in himself experiences which the artist felt—either of the outer or inner world—and that these experiences are taken by the artist as such—that is to say at their face value before the analytical intellect has broken them up into scientific categories or the moral judgment separated them into its categories. Mr. Abercrombie's main departure from Croce is that whereas Croce recognizes only expression in the inner sense of the word—that is to say regards the work of art as essentially completed when imaged in the artist's mind and the technical expression as only a sort of memoria technica—Abercrombie regards the artistic impulse as essentially motor and calling for outer expression to the end that it be shared: this outer expression Mr. Abercrombie calls publication, and he differs from Croce by saying that no work of art exists before publication, in that sense, is made.

And where Croce is interested only in the philosophy of the matter, Abercrombie translates the whole thing into terms of human life and gives us really an eclectic theory of art, using the insight of others to complete his total picture of the artistic activity. Summed up, what he tells us amounts to this: that all experience when we take it as such, for its intrinsic interest, may be called aesthetic experience but is not always in point of fact beautiful experience.

162

First Impressions

When some part of this experience appeals especially to one with the artist's endowment, when, for him, it is expressive, he seeks by the use of the appropriate medium to put down certain symbols which, on our reading, seeing, or hearing them, will reproduce in us an experience corresponding to his original aesthetic experience: this latter experience is now no longer aesthetic only, but artistic. What symbols will convey it—or, to be more accurate, reproduce a corresponding experience—is a matter of empirical discovery. The artist's chief task is to separate from his aesthetic experience all that is alien to it: for in life we have little if any aesthetic experience in a pure state: practical or moral ends and the contingent are always mixed up with it, diluting or destroying it. Form, in the work of art, is simply the symbol of this banishment from the experience of all that is non-aesthetic, for the chief characteristic of form is unity and every work of art must have unity: that is to say it must contain no element which is not strictly necessary to express part of the experience, and the experience itself must be a unified one, for our very consciousness itself insists upon unity: a divided consciousness is a self-contradiction in terms and in fact means a neurosis or a split personality.

And while, in practical life, we have to put up with mixed and incompatible experiences—have to deal with chaotic situations—Mr. Abercrombie gives the simple example of our missing trains, which is a sort of insult to our rationality—we insist, in our mental life upon something better than that: upon having experience which wholly satisfies because it all hangs together, the parts being interdependent and a whole which, as a whole, can be imaginatively held and enjoyed. And it is for this reason, he tells us, that in art we even enjoy tragedy, the subject matter of which in real life would revolt us. For in art we do not see this subject matter as we see it in life—a something merely dreadful, as a murder, for example. But we see it as something which, given its elements, is inevitable. It all hangs together. And we enjoy the inevitability, despite the hurts involved, simply because this interdependence of one thing on another, this strict reasonableness, this wholeness and oneness of experience is the deepest desire of our mind. And it is in this sense that Mr. Abercrombie interprets Bacon's saying that in poetry we have "the shows of things submitted to the desires of the mind"—in that sense and not in the careless sense that some people would give it that poetry dealt in comfortable things: for comfortable things would not be the desire of the mind but of the senses.

And on the basis of this theory Mr. Abercrombie even ventures to restore that venerable and Platonic phrase absolute beauty. Perhaps as a speculative possibility rather than as, for us, a fact. But, he tells us the word beauty, in its strict sense is simply the name for the state of mind of one who judges that expression has been successful, beauty is a judgment just as truth is. And, if a possible god could see the universe at once on the aesthetic level, could envisage it all as pure experience, see it in every part inter-dependent, with all that is to us contingent and chaotic seen to fit in, to belong, to be necessary to the functioning of the whole, that experience of that being would be an experience of absolute beauty.

But for us, art alone can give the experience of beauty because art is the only realm in which man can fully realize that state of unity to which, in all other planes of living he can only strive, and that at a distance, to approximate.

The Poetry and Criticism of
T. Sturge Moore

IN the days of Emerson and Carlyle, Americans were
not afraid to adopt English masters in the realm of the
spirit and Englishmen could return the compliment.
Even as recently as the days of Meredith we could
give a man a hearing, and profit from him, even where
his own countrymen failed in some measure to do so
themselves.

To-day we seem more narrowly nationalistic in
literary matters, and although our younger generation
likes to quote De Gourmont it is rare to find a poet
or thinker of another country having a following in
America. But then the days of discipleship itself
seem to have vanished. Where now are such writers
as Walter Pater, addressing themselves to discussion
of the values of life and finding in a large number of
men younger than themselves an eager response and
a following?

Yet there are still such men writing, and there is
still need for the expression of those values in life and
conduct which are at once philosophical and aesthetic
but which come outside the boundary lines of the
special disciplines which are being unduly popularized

to-day: sentimental radicalism and psychoanalysis. But whereas the Paters had a public that was perhaps too enthusiastic in its discipleship these later men find no such recognition: though they do not lack for recognition by a public fit and few.

I say "these men" but I do not think of very many. Perhaps T. Sturge Moore stands alone at the present time in that class which has included the artist and the thinker together: the Goethe-type as one might call it. It is the class in which many would place, for instance, Mr. Santayana, although he is perhaps too much the professional philosopher and the defender of a certain doctrine—even if no one quite knows what it is—to be altogether trusted by those people who have to live in the world and who therefore ask a certain worldliness in their teachers.

If discipleship of any kind were fashionable to-day, T. Sturge Moore would undoubtedly have a large following in America, for he meets us half way in some of our American attitudes and is yet able to save us from the Philistinism resulting from our interpretation of them. We distrust, for example, the artist and the critic who talks about art for art's sake. We prefer to talk of art for life's sake. In Mr. Moore's theory of the relation of aesthetics to life we should find fulfilled our demand that art should have some vital relationship to life but the fulfillment would be on honest terms —not a giving in to our Philistinism which can see art only as a hand-maid of ethics.

167

First Impressions

While the vice of our popular poetry is rhetoric our professional philosophers go to the other extreme. They are anti-rhetorical, even banishing the logos and making philosophy a matter of empiricism. Two extremes and both bad, perhaps. But Mr. Moore expresses in his poetry a sort of radical empiricism which is very refreshing after the traditional Platonism of the English poets—a Platonism which has become very thin in the course of the years and which itself is likely to lead to rhetoric.

It seems to me that the solid empirical character of Mr. Moore's poetry and his theories of art both spring from his primary occupation—that of a wood engraver. We have had painter poets and it is not hard to see the influence of their painting on their poetry. But wood-engraving is a very different thing from painting. It cannot be improvised; it has to make the best of a difficult medium; it must feel, in the doing, more the conscious work of one's own hands; and it requires greater self-control, technically, on the part of the artist.

Mr. Moore's thought, both his critical thought and his lyrical thought, always seems to me that of a man who has learned his world by touching first the things around him. And we shall see later how literally true this is of his poetry.

First, however, let us look at his critical attitude. Like all modern men he sees that the universe eludes any formulation of it that we may make, and he sees

168

very clearly the grounds for that despair that some poets and some philosophers have voiced. But he also sees that even though the universe as such may be conceived of as evil there are some good things in it. We may cherish and enlarge these good things. Therefore the chief human virtue is hope. For only through hope can we go on with what is certainly our human task—even if it be only a self-appointed human task—of spreading the good.

By good Mr. Moore does not mean anything that has to be defined or argued over in a class in ethics. It does not matter, he says, if a child thinks a diamond makes light. When the child says something that would imply that the diamond makes light we know that he is speaking the truth: for he is reporting a valid experience. It is so with our use of the word good.

The expressionist and the "formal" schools of aesthetics agree in saying that art has nothing to do with morals: that a work of art is a thing that pleases in and for itself because it expresses for us an emotion, and that to bend a work of art to the task of teaching a lesson is to inject a practical issue—in Croce's use of the word practical—into it, and so destroy its artistic value. To that our public, aesthetically rather blind anyway, replies that a work of art which does not teach a moral lesson is a waste of time or a sensual indulgence or an incomprehensible piece of abracadabra. Mr. Moore stands apart from these extremes. In the sense that art must teach a lesson he is against the moralist, for he remarks somewhere that the imaginations of the artist may body forth some thing that in "real life" may not be reached for hundreds of years. Even when a work of art uses moral ideas or situations as its material we must not ask for a direct bearing on daily life. In "The Best Poetry," the last paper in his recent book, "Some Soldier Poets," he tells us:

I mentioned that some of the best poetry has been charged with immorality. Such accusations are usually made by people who regard the fact that poets can and often do preach excellent sermons as the only excuse for verse. Now to elucidate this difficulty we must conceive of English morality as something dependent upon the customs and habits of the English, not as an absolute criterion of worth. In practical life it is a mistake to run counter to one's neighbors without a weighty reason, without being prepared to suffer as a consequence. But in the realm of contemplation, whither poetry should lift us, morality, instead of being established, is a project.

There, if it is not to prove futile, neither deed nor doer must be left unconsidered, but the whole reality must be harmoniously reviewed. For this reason we should welcome all who can give literary form to any accident, however inconvenient that accident may be in a mundane sphere. . . .

On the other hand this contemplation is not the divorced from life sort of thing described by such a formalist as Clive Bell who tells us that pictures are aesthetically validated by their "significant form" which has nothing to do with their representative quality but which is a sort of pure geometry of the soul—and only the contemplative soul at that. As against that idea Mr. Moore says in the introduction to his little book on "Altdorfer":

What are the master motives that should govern the painting of pictures? . . . Other some there are who cry, the desire to improve others and one's self. Now, although Ruskin has been much decried, this does appear a worthy motive; the improvement is so obviously needed. Yet unfortunately there are a mulitude of ways in which we could bear improving, and apparently little reason for preference of betterment by means of art. Have the great artists been those who most strenuously strove to improve others or even themselves? Have they not rather shown a tendency to be contented by advancing art? Lastly, what improvement is it that does result from art? These questions, except the last, leave me utterly in the lurch; but for that last I find an answer on the tip of my tongue: Beauty improves by educing elevation, delicacy, and refinement, and it also exhilarates; and in Greece, and even once or twice since, you might have found whole companies that would have stared at you, if you had suggested that art had any other business than the discovery and revelation of the beautiful.

And now can we not reform this demand that art should seek to improve, by saying, that art seeks to reveal beauty, and that contemplation of beauty exhilarates, refines, and elevates? Reveal beauty! that, then, is for the artist the sovereign com-

171

mand. Contemplate beauty! obedience to that is for all men
a prime assistance towards exhilaration, refinement, elevation;
and what more do we need?

One practical consequence of Croce's doctrine of
beauty as expression, a doctrine to which, of course
Mr. Moore is not hospitable, has been individualistic
impressionism in art: the cult of the spontaneous; a
desire to give one's artistic productions to the world in
what may be called their first state; a hostility to
revision on the ground that it will blur or falsify
the first expression and lead to artificiality. The consequence is not a logical one, however, for any revision of the outer form of expression is *ipso facto* a
revision of the intuition, a freeing of it from some
practical or other irrelevant matter. And as a critic
and a practising artist Mr. Moore is quite aware that
first impressions are not the best and purest, and
individual idiosyncracy is not the material of valuable
art. I do not know whether he blames the Crocean
doctrine for these consequences, although it sounds
as if he did when he tells us—in his "Albert Dürer"
—that his view of art is neither the "scientific" one
nor the "personal theory that reduces art to an
expression of, and an appeal to, individual temper-
aments." But I think myself that his views are
perfectly reconcilable to those of Croce, and, as for
the personal temperament, has not Havelock Ellis said
somewhere that the man who is perfectly true to his

individual self to-day will be called typical in years to come? But Mr. Moore sets up for all of us an ideal in aesthetics. He proceeds to say that his position "is the assertion of the sovereignty of the aesthetic conscience on exactly the same grounds as sovereignty is claimed for the moral conscience. Aesthetics deals with the morality of appeals addressed to the senses. That is, it estimates the success of such appeals in regard to the promotion of fuller and more harmonious life."

But this must be read in the light of what we have already quoted on the freedom of art from direct moral concerns and it may even better be understood in the light of his quotation from Mr. Moore's most important book of aesthetic theory, his "Art and Life," in which he builds from the actual examples of the lives and work of Flaubert and of Blake:

Socialists [or he might have said, American captains of industry and statesmen] might do well to regard the professions of religion, music, painting, and poetry as asylums for the over-sensitive, which today they practically are. Even the doll-like functions of dwelling in pretty houses and wearing fine clothes might prove worth more than they cost.

This is not the only time that he couples art and religion. Indeed he has already brought them together in his use of the common word conscience, and in the prolegomena to his discussion of the work of Dürer he speaks of the sense of proportion in human

173

life: the desire for harmonious development of the faculties, the spiritual necessity of making our reason prevail against brute fact, ending with these grave words:

For my own part, those appear to me the grandest characters who, on finding that there is no other purchase for effort but only hope, and they can never cease from hope but by ceasing to live, clear their minds of all idle acquiescence in what could never be hoped, and concentrate their energies on conquering whatever in their own nature, and in the world about them, militates against their most essential character— reason, which seeks always to give a higher value to life.

And having thus spoken he proceeds:

When we speak of the sense of proportion displayed in the design of a building, many will think that the word is used in quite a different sense, and one totally unrelated to those which I have been discussing. But no; life and art are parallel and correspond throughout; ethics are the aesthetics of life, religion is the art of living. Taste and conscience only differ in their provinces, not in their procedure. Both are based on instinctive preferences; the canon of either is merely so many of those preferences as, by their constant recurrence to individuals gifted with the power of drawing others after them, are widely accepted. The preference of serenity to melancholy, of light to darkness, are among the most firmly established in the canon, that is all. The sense of proportion within a design is employed to stimulate and delight the eye. Ordinary people may fear there is some

174

abstruse science about this. Not at all; it is as simple as relishing milk and honey, and its development an exact parallel to the training of the palate to distinguish the flavors of teas, coffees, and wines. "Taste and see" is the whole business.

One practical suggestion that Mr. Moore makes to artists as a result of his aesthetic views is that they should cherish originality less and perfection more, and specifically that they should not fear to rewrite master-pieces when poised, so to speak, on the vantage ground of the original artist's achievement they see not only its beauties but its failures: a thesis which he develops in a brochure entitled "Hark to These Three," a sort of modern symposium on the production of works of art.

But we must leave the aesthetician for the poet and the seer. When I called Mr. Moore an empiricist among poets I did not mean an empiricist in the sense of an anti-intellectualist, but rather that he was an inductionist rather than a deductionist, an anti-Platonic philosopher. Indeed in one poem published in an English periodical he specifically declares himself on the matter. The universe may contain glorious things, he says, that we know nothing of, but he adds:

> Not that I can, like scornful Plato, fear
> Our fine things but poor copies of true worth;
> Proportioned to this earth,
> There thrill and shape small genuine glories here.

175

First Impressions

And as a poet Mr. Moore begins with the smallest of them. To him the world that matters is a world that we have built—and as a wood engraver he knows that we don't build by merely making blue prints and computations. In his book of child poems, "The Little School," he tells us:

> Sing, for with hands,
> One thumb and four fingers apiece,
> They built the temples of Egypt and Greece!
> Sing, for in many lands
> Are things of use and beauty seen
> That without hands had never been—
> Without skilled hands.

While there is, too, an aesthetic of touch:

> Joy steals through me if I sleek
> Damask petals of a rose
> Softer than a fairy's cheek;
> While for gladness my hand goes
> Through fringes of floss-silk and guesses
> How slowly mermaids comb their tresses . . .

All of Mr. Moore's poetry seems to begin with something bodily, often prosaic, and to carry it up an aerial ladder. Our meals for instance, are apt to be prosaic affairs, although a meal may be a eucharist. But see how the ascent from that hearty, naïve joy in food of the child, right up to highest poetry is made in a poem of four stanzas that any child will read with understanding and delight:

First Impressions

BEAUTIFUL MEALS

How nice it is to eat!
All creatures love it so,
That they who first did spread,
Ere breaking bread,
A cloth like level snow,
Were right, I know.

And they were wise and sweet
Who, glad that meats taste good,
Used speech in an arch style,
And oft would smile
To raise the cheerful mood,
While at their food.

And those who first, so neat,
Placed knife and fork so straight,
The glass on the right hand;
And all, as planned,
Each day set round the plate,—
Be their praise great!

For then, their hearts being light,
They plucked hedge-posies bright—
Flowers who, their scent being sweet,
Give nose and eye a treat:
'Twas they, my heart can tell,
Not eating fast, but well,
Who wove the spell
Which finds me every day,

And makes each meal-time gay;
I know 'twas they.

If there be any adult reader who thinks that that
is too naïve to be a real poem let him try it on some
children—but surely its poetic quality is evident.

Many of Mr. Moore's poems, as might be expected,
are philosophic. Two of the most beautiful of them, I
think, are his lines addressed to Rabindranath Tagore
and his poem to Leopardi. The former I may quote
in full—indeed its sentences are so long that one could
not quote it in part. One critic—made insensitive
possibly by the fact that he had a dogmatic religion to
fall back on—told me once he could see nothing in this
poem, but I think it is an almost matchless example
of the expression of an attitude difficult enough to
express anyway, and here poetically realized. Certainly there is no obscurity in it:

I cannot mock thy "Yes" with "No";
For what is hidden may be of such worth
As beggars all we know:
Yet how mine wonders at thy mind!—
To see schooled man so easy on this earth
And yet not blind!
Is it true thy candour weighs
Long June days,
Deep clear nights,
Full tenderness on self-forgetful face,
All-probing knowledge, art perfection-nigh,
And aught else that delights

178

First Impressions

Poor man's goodwill
As being really like a trace
Left on fingers that have touched,—
Perhaps half-tried to kill,—
Some lustrous butterfly?
Is Psyche so much grander than our sages vouched?
That all our noblest win of her is like
A few scales brushed from a cerulean wing?
Ah, is all evil impotent to strike
Her blow more damaging
Than clumsy child adorer gives the fly
That he admires too much
To really clutch,
Although he fain must try?
And, if he woo,
Will she even dare much too,
Hover down to his lips and, like his rapture returned,
Enter and home in the brain and the heart that for her
    yearned?

And turning from the optimist to the pessimist,
Mr. Moore compares the cold and frozen thought of
Leopardi to the moon:

> Yes, thy thought ached, it was so cold;
> And winsome movement, and choice sound,
> In harmonies, divinely wrought,
> Could they be born of that profound
> Despair which they so clearly taught?

And then he turns the tables of Leopardi's own
beauty upon him: for that cold moon to which he has

179

compared him is only visible to us by virtue of the rays
of the warm sun which it reflects:

> So in the beauty of thine odes
> Man's glowing, eager spirit shines . . .

—a really valid criticism of any pretensions to absolute
pessimism that are uttered by any poet. But Mr.
Moore's avoidance of pessimism is not by a mere
logical turning of tables. He sees the pessimist's
point and he sees that under certain circumstances it
is a valid one. Only by a certain faith—by his oft
stressed virtue of hope—can the sensitive man avoid
it. Here is part of a poem, "Dark Days," from a series
of his shorter books bound in one and published under
the title of "Poems" (London: Duckworth):

> Only if fact can answer reason's prayer
> Both in one life and all,
> And in resultant beauty souls be good;
> Only if toward that goal each day we fare,
> And never stand below where we have stood
> Answer I to your call,
> Ye stars, or yours, ye flowers of field or wood.
>
> Yet is all vain? vain then this sad surmise;
> For still unknown our doom;
> Yet we have fancies, can enchant our eyes,
> Paint bliss upon the gloom;
>
> We have some strength, though it be not enough
> The vast whole to transform;

It can spread lawns where yet the waste is rough,
Some blossom shield from storm;

Our strength can make fair skies its harvest fields,
And glean from cloud and star;
The grace of trees, the calm of distant hills
Garner, and add what every flower yields
To feed a beauty and a light that fills
Our eyes, when those eyes are
Glad to see other eyes forget life's ills.

The greatest ill of all—if we can say that death is
that—Mr. Moore dominates imaginatively by this same
concrete method. He has again no Platonic or other
mystical recipe. He meditates "On Death" in this
same volume and again uses what we may call the case
method. After an introductory stanza confessing that
"Self-questioned ignorance yields no reply" he goes
over the actual deaths of our fellow-men which we
know from history, memoirs, and gossip. How did
they die? How to themselves they died we cannot
tell; we can only tell how to us they seemed to die,
but the upshot of the matter is that:

Imagination must teach us how to die,
Must age and death enhance
And give to each a value clear and high:—
Or fail and leave us to blank ignorance.

So far I have quoted only what might be called
philosophical poems, but Mr. Moore is an aesthetic
poet as well as a thinking one, and has for his own

181

heart's country a land that is at once beautiful and rugged, a sort of imaginative sublimation of the home of many of our human values, Greece. It is the Greece not of fact but of legend and its typical inhabitant is the Centaur about whom some of Mr. Moore's poems are written—and some of his prose poems, while he has made a beautiful prose translation of de Guerin's "The Centaur and the Bacchante." The first poem in the volume mentioned above is a delightful dialogue between two male Centaurs, the harried last of their kind, one of whom, going forth to kidnap a woman, brings back instead a child—that they may rear him in their own scale of values which is a high and hard one, free from human sentimentality: although there is humor as well as beauty in the poem when the older Centaur, censorious at first, at this wild idea of his mate's, begins to fall in love with the child and to prophesy of his future, the while they both play with him:

> Toss him back to these arms,
> Like a bird through the air, he is caught.
> Oh! he shall run naked
> Till hairs on him grow,
> And he shall climb mountains
> And trample their snow
> Till hooves on him grow!
> Till hooves on him grow!

And in "The Sea is Kind"—the title-poem to a collection of Mr. Moore's work published in America—

we have a beautiful seaside country and a shepherd who yearns for a greater task, who feels the sea in his blood:

> Thou knowest, Menalcas,
> I built my hut not sheltered but exposed,
> Round, not right-angled.
> A separate window like a mouth to breathe,
> No matter whence the breeze might blow,—
> A separate window like an eye to watch
> From off the headland lawn that prompting wink
> Of Ocean musing "Why" whenever he
> May glimpse me at some pitiable task.

and who does, under the patronage of a nymph, find the sea kind—but kind because he is adequate to its demands on strength and courage.

A number of these poems retell the ancient myths, often from some new and delightful point of view, and always with a sort of picturesque and kindly wisdom—for even wisdom may be picturesque. We have a rendering of the Eros and Psyche story from the point of view of Pan who rescues Psyche, and we meet Theseus and Medea. The last poem is a beautiful study in sombre coloring. Medea is weaving the poisoned robe:

> This have I woven, this my needle wrought
> Slowly to beauty,—as thy Spring adorns,
> Fold after fold, a rich and worthy land—
> With leaves of varied shapes, with tints of green

183

First Impressions

More subtly diverse than the lyre's notes,
With blossoms of a flute-like rapturous hue,
Sheer bliss in blue, in pink or purple sobs,
Deep drone of reds and saffrons, shouts of gold:
And not content with this, but god-like still,—
Since through the dusky inwards of the wood
Between the branches, wings the feathered life
Whose rapid pulse astonishes the hand
Of ill-shod mortals trudging after joy,—
I have portrayed tit, finch, or crested wren,
Flashing athwart each sombre interspace
My broidered wreaths encircled; but the snake,
The silent pole-cat, fierce red ant, the wasp,—
These though my thoughts were like them, are not here.
Yet what is here might make the forest groan,
To think its wizard influence had failed
Impress on any life a character
So secretly dread, though framed to almost please,—
This brown rich like the burnt cheek of a stone
Squared to be plinth unto some column grand;
Near which the masons light a little fire,
Whereat to broil their salt-fried fish in lard,
When o'er the cockling scales and stiff-ribbed fins,
Again, such browns mingled with golds, blue dusk,
And silver scorched, increase beneath the heat;
While sometimes, in the afternoon, a storm,
Parting his heavy indigo palls of rain,
Will show such browns above the sulphurous west;—
This brown, the dye in which I souse my web,
Is color of poison; and for this is veiled
The light which else would make my chamber bland . . .

First Impressions

That is not only a remarkable piece of color painting but the hyperaesthesia by which Medea sees her brown, the color of her poison, repeated in image after image of the daily life, is dramatically fine as well as decorative.

Indeed Mr. Moore is a dramatist, although space forbids any consideration of his work in that kind. I must mention, however, "Tragic Mothers" (London: Grant Richards), in which he uses that old new form, the "Noh play" adapted from the Japanese by Mr. Yeats and particularly meant, in its new form, for presentation by masked actors in a drawing-room or other space where there is no stage nor scenery but simply a curtain folded and refolded between scenes and intermissions.

I think I have said enough, however, to show that in T. Sturge Moore we have a man who deserves disciples. His aesthetic theories are his own and do justice to all the interests involved: to artist as well as to public and certainly to the moral issue in that aesthetic controversy which seems to go on and on. For our own times he is both a tonic and an anodyne: avoiding both the extremes of the men who put all their eggs into the one basket of social reform or Socialism or some form of political radicalism, and the less admirable extreme of the man who flees to an ivory tower—and indeed anyone who has read Mr. Moore's "Danaë" and seen how her brass tower was no protection, may well doubt whether an ivory tower

185

First Impressions

would be any better. Yet we do need a refuge and
Mr. Moore's mythical Greek uplands are as beautiful
as and more bracing than the refuges of almost any
other English poet. As countries of the mind they
are more interesting than Morris's Earthly Paradise
and less monotonous than Spenser's enchanted forests.
Though remote they have a salty tang of real life
in them.

I have mentioned a few of his books by title, but
the following notes, which do not pretend to be a complete bibliography, may be of use to the reader. They
do not include his books issued in limited editions
by the Vale or Eragny Presses. His first volume
of poems "The Vine Dresser and Other Poems" was
published—as were one or two poetic dramas—by the
Unicorn Press in 1899. Most of these poems were
reprinted in "The Sea is Kind" (Houghton Mifflin:
1914.) The volume "Poems" included work originally published from 1903 to 1904, and has not been
reprinted in America or in England since that date.
"The Little School" originally printed by the Eragny
Press with woodcuts by the author is included in "The
Sea is Kind" and is also issued separately in this country as was "Some Soldier Poets"—a volume of
criticism in which Mr. Moore does justice to his subject as poets even when that involves admitting that
a hero may not always be a perfect poet. And that
book contains a splendid essay on the recognition of
"The Best Poetry." Two books of dramatic and semi-

186

dramatic poetry, "A Sicilian Idyll and Judith" and "Marianne" were published by Duckworth, London, in 1911. "Tragic Mothers" was published by Grant Richards in 1920 and the "The Powers of the Air" a colloquy, in prose and verse, on art, laid in ancient Athens, in the same year. And coming from poetry to criticism we have Altdorfer (Unicorn Press, in 1900, "Dürer" (Duckworth) 1904, "Correggio" (Duckworth) 1906, "Art and Life" (Methuen) 1910, "Hark to these Three" (Elkin Matthews) 1915; and the above mentioned "Some Soldier Poets" in 1919.

But a bibliography is a dull thing to end with, so here, for colophon, is a short lyric of our poet's, a lyric that seems to catch in words a music as of a violin, a poem of unrealistic matter, of pure emotion:

THE DYING SWAN

O silver-throated Swan
Struck, struck! a golden dart
Clean through thy breast has gone
Home to thy heart.
Thrill, thrill, O silver throat!
O silver trumpet, pour
Love for defiance back
Of him who smote!
And brim, brim o'er
With love; and ruby-dye thy track
Down thy last living reach

First Impressions

Of river, sail the golden light—
Enter the sun's heart—even teach,
O wondrous-gifted Pain, teach thou
The God to love, let him learn how!

And to the reader whose taste is genuine the slight
colloquialism of that final phrase will not only be
recognized as something typical of Mr. Moore but
something that by its very unpretentiousness completes
the beauty of that most moving song.

The Poetry of Alice Meynell

In the obituary notices of Alice Meynell there was
again revealed what had occasionally been noticeable
in criticisms of her work—a certain grudgingness. She
was taken, perhaps, too literally at her own over
modest valuation as a poet of a single mood, and perhaps those critics who were not themselves of her religious faith thought that she sometimes sang the hymns
of a single church rather than songs of universal
interest. This, of course was not the case at all,
although our prevalent confusion between poetry and
doctrine has caused many people to misunderstand both
Alice Meynell and her *protégé* Francis Thompson—
who was referred to by Austin Harrison in the English
Review, when his collected poems appeared, as "a
reed-pipe of neo-mediævalism . . . a poet of the gar-
goyle" and out of sympathy, therefore, with our own
century. But poetry, as Lascelles Abercrombie has
so finely said, is written in an eternal present tense:
what dates in it is not essentially poetry; and we might
add that it is never doctrinal. The fact that Mrs.
Meynell is a Roman Catholic, from the point of view
of her poetry, simply amounts to this: that she has had
certain spiritual experiences which we, her readers,
may or may not have had, but which, in any event,

she will describe in a terminology which differs from
that which Mr. Thomas Hardy or the Sitwells would
use in their poetry—and which, by its very difference,
makes for a more clear-cut and fresh presentation,
gives us old emotions, perhaps, but experienced from
a different angle. Let us suppose that we believe,
theoretically, in the brotherhood of man—if indeed
after the war such belief is at all possible to anyone—
or at least that we pay tribute to some idea of human
solidarity, but do not feel it concretely enough to
become very excited over the matter. Let us then
turn to Mrs. Meynell's poem, "The Unknown God."
Let, also, the good evangelical or the conscientiously
free-thinking reader forget any prejudices that he may
cherish against the theology and the ceremonies of the
Roman Catholic church. Then let him read:

> One of the crowd went up
> And knelt before the Paten and the cup,
> Received the Lord, returned in peace, and prayed
> Close to my side: then in my heart I said:
>
> "O Christ, in this man's life—
> This stranger who is Thine—in all his strife,
> All his felicity, his good and ill,
> In the assaulted stronghold of his will,
>
> "I do confess Thee near
> Within this lonely conscience, closed away
> Within this brother's solitary day.

First Impressions

"Christ in his unknown heart,
His intellect unknown—this love, this art,
This battle and this peace, this destiny
That I shall never know, look upon me!

"Christ in his numbered breath,
Christ in his beating heart and in his death,
Christ in his mystery! From that secret place
And from that separate dwelling, give me grace!"

Again, the spectacle of a general communion gives
Mrs. Meynell inspiration for a poem the last two
stanzas of which apply equally to the secular and
evolutionary view of man's destiny and salvation as
they do to the ecclesiastical, and the last stanza of
which is most suggestive in the light it throws upon
the puzzling discrepancy between the littleness of man
and the unlimited material vast in which he finds himself a floating speck:

I saw this people as a field of flowers,
Each grown at such a price
The sun of unimaginable powers
Did no more than suffice.

A thousand single central daisies they,
A thousand of the one:
For each, the entire monopoly of day:
For each, the whole of the devoted sun.

Already it will be seen that Mrs. Meynell is the
poet of what may be called spiritual paradox—not the

crude paradox in which Mr. Chesterton indulges but
the sober and true paradox which is implicit in the
very nature of human consciousness itself, that union
of the one in the many, that play of opposites and
reconciliation of contradictions. Perhaps, indeed, that
paradox extends to the constitution of the world itself and will yet confound the mechanists and the be-
haviorists who would make of consciousness an epi-
phenomenon. Bergson is not alone in thinking that,
and it may surprise some readers to find in a poet they
expected, on the superficial evidence of her language,
to be Roman Catholic exclusively, writing a poem which
is a thing of beauty and also a neat rendering of
the Bergsonian idea of the world as a cosmic com-
promise between matter and spirit, a modus vivendi
the operation of which would seem totally different
to us if we viewed it from the side of the *élan vital*
rather than from the side of space and matter. Here
is the poem, "To a Daisy," and the similarity to the
Bergsonian point of view is very evident:

> Slight as thou art, thou art enough to hide
> Like all created things, secrets from me,
> And stand a barrier to eternity.
> And I, how can I praise thee well and wide
>
> From where I dwell—upon the hither side?
> Thou little veil for so great mystery,
> When shall I penetrate all things and thee,
> And then look back? For this I must abide,

192

First Impressions

Till thou shalt grow and fold and be unfurled
Literally between me and the world.
Then shall I drink from in beneath a spring,

And from a poet's side shall read his book,
O daisy mine, what will it be to look
From God's side even of such a simple thing?

That sense of restrained paradox runs throughout
Mrs. Meynell's work, and her religious phraseology
is particularly well fitted to convey it to us. "The
Young Neophyte" is a beautiful sonnet enshrining
the fatefulness of every human action, the gift of
the full flower that is implicit in the gift of the bud,
the preparation we are constantly making for crises
which are yet hidden in the future. "Thoughts in
Separation" also deals with the paradoxical overcoming
of the handicaps of personal absence of our friends
through community of thought and feeling. Not only
are these paradoxes in human psychology delicately
set forth by the poet, but those darker ones of human
work and destiny are consolingly illuminated in such
a poem as "Builders of Ruins"—its very title is at
once a summary of human effort and a poem—and
the poem does not at all depend for its effect, its
consolation, upon anything foreign to its poetic truth.

Just what is meant by poetic truth may be illustrated
from the one poem in all of Mrs. Meynell's collection
that has a dubious sound, that does not present us
the true, the realizable side of religion (which Matthew

Arnold was so anxious that poetry should conserve), but with the debatable, the theological, the side that is not in the present tense. Indeed, the poem may stand as an illustrious warning against confusing real poetry—in whose truth we need not be afraid to trust just because its author does not inhabit our own thought world—with versified theology, philosophy or ethics or politics. If all of Mrs. Meynell's poetry were so doctrinally limited and parochial as her "Messina 1908," then, indeed, her appeal would be limited and parochial. It is a commentary on the Messina earthquake and upon the aspect of it that transcends the immediate knowledge which is the basis of poetry. For that matter, the question of the relation of any possible God to the human situation involved in such a catastrophe transcends our philosophy. And even in religious circles the idea of a theodicy, of a world governed by a personal God and governed from more or less of a human viewpoint, has been pushed into the background. Indeed, such a god considered alone never did "make good." Some mediator, Christ or the Saints, always did have to intervene between man and such divinity. And it is precisely in the one case where Mrs. Meynell tries to present the governing rather than the immanent God to us that she fails— as, if poetry be realization of concrete experience, we should expect her to fail. The first stanza of the poem, addressed to the Deity, describes in a few bold

strokes the wreck of Messina, and ends with the
lines:

> Destroyer, we have cowered beneath Thine own
> Immediate unintelligible hand.

The second stanza describes the missions of mercy to
the stricken city, and ends:

> . . . Our shattered fingers feel
> Thy mediate and intelligible hand.

The essential weakness of this dependence for
structure and effect upon the two adjectives and their
negatives is no less obvious than the poet's attribu-
tion of such apparently impulsive and then retrac-
tatory conduct to a God whose ways must either be
explicable in terms of a human sense of order or not
be made the subject of human discourse at all.

One of the subtlest of the parodoxes which Mrs.
Meynell expresses is that in the relation of the human
spirit to time. It is seen in her "Length of Days"
addressed to "the early dead in battle" and more
sharply in "Time's Reversals: A Daughter's Paradox," a poem based on the fact that "Dr. Johnson out-
lived by thirty years his wife, who was twenty years his
senior":

To his devoted heart
  Who, young, had loved his aging mate for life,

First Impressions

In late lone years Time gave the elder's part,
   Time gave the bridegroom's boast,
   Time gave a younger wife.

A wilder prank and plot
   Time soon will promise, threaten, offering me
Impossible things that Nature suffers not—
   A daughter's riper mind, a child's seniority.

O by my filial tears
   Mourned all too young, Father. On this my head
Time will yet force at last the longer years,
   Claiming some strange respect for me from you, the dead.

Nay, nay! Too new to know
   Time's conjuring is, too great to understand.
Memory has not died: it leaves me so—
   Leaning a fading brow on your unfaded hand.

It has been remarked more than once that Mrs. Meynell's essays are often about beautiful perceptions, while her poems always have something in them of the essay, some expression of thought, but this latter is never mere thinking: it, too, is always a direct perception. And it is never sentimental thought. This child of an old faith quite aware of all the movements of life is at home, too, in her own century. In "The Threshing Machine" she repeats but to dismiss what would be the conventional lament at machinery taking the place of the fan and flail—those objects made sacred by their associations with the parable of God sifting out the chaff from the wheat—the very lament, in fact, that Ruskin lifted:

> The unbreathing engine marks no tune,
> Steady at sunrise, steady at noon,
>   Inhuman, perfect, saving time,
>   And saving measure and saving rhyme—
> And did our Ruskin speak too soon?
>
> "No noble strength on earth" he sees
> "Save Hercules' arm"; his grave decrees
> Curse wheel and steam. As the wheels ran
> I saw the other strength of man,
> I knew the brain of Hercules.

But it would be unjust to give the impression that all of Mrs. Meynell's poetry is that of "wit" or metaphysic. Both as a critic and as a poet her perceptions are exquisite, and no other poet of her day has approached her in the matter of perfection of form. Read almost any of her poems slowly and attentively and you will receive the impression of something that is delicate in form and tracery, without an iota of waste material in it, but all done in a medium so resilient, so strong, that we can well imagine it lasting forever—fine carving, but in an incorruptible metal. While it is not very often that Mrs. Meynell paints, say, a landscape for its own sake or indulges in anything so obvious as the usual sort of onomatopœia, let the reader turn to her early poem "The Lady Poverty" with the last stanza:

197

First Impressions

Where is her ladyhood? Not here,
Not among modern kinds of men:
But in the stony fields where clear
Through the thin trees the skies appear,
In delicate spare soil and fen,
And slender landscape and austere.

An etcher's landscape, but what etcher could have done in so few strokes such a picture as that, with the very rhythm of the lines, and the necessary pauses between the words, and their melody, all making the actual picture: and showing, incidentally, the falsity of Lessing's idea that poetry should leave to painting the depiction of spatial things and confine itself to action.

Before ending with the quotation of a late poem that might well be considered the most beautiful Mrs. Meynell has written, we may look for a moment at one kind of poem she has written, a kind which is always interesting when it comes from a major artist: the poem about poetry.

Mrs. Meynell has not only written in "The Courts: A Figure of the Epiphany," a beautiful statement of the ultimate simplicity of real poetry:

The poet's imageries are noble ways,
Approaches to a plot, an open shrine . . .

And yet the open heavenward plot, with dew,
Ultimate poetry, inclosed, enskyed,

(Albeit such ceremonies lead thereto),
Stands on the yonder side.
Plain, behind oracles, it is; and past
All symbols, simple; perfect, heavenly-wild,
The song some loaded poets reach at last—
The kings that found a Child.

—but she has seen that the very laws of metre themselves are living things which move with joy and reverence the poet who really sees and feels what they can do for him. Hence the simplicity that she has hymned is not a simplicity of anarchism in language, of muttering every fancy in the very words with which it came to birth, but a simplicity in an ordered medium. And so she also, in a much later poem, sings:

THE LAWS OF VERSE

Dear laws, come to my breast!
  Take all my frame, and make your close arms meet
Around me; and so ruled, so warmed, so pressed,
  I breathe, aware; I feel my wild heart beat.

Dear laws, be wings to me!
The feather merely floats. O be it heard
Through weight of life—the skylark's gravity—
That I am not a feather, but a bird.

And a few pages farther on in the last section of her book we have a poem on "The English Metres," in which the same idea is treated even more prosodically:

199

First Impressions

The rooted liberty of flowers in breeze
  Is theirs, by national luck impulsive, terse,
Tethered, uncaptured, rules obeyed "at ease"
  Time-strengthened laws of verse.

Or they are like our seasons that admit
  Inflexion, not infraction: Autumn hoar,
Winter more tender than our thoughts of it,
  But a year's steadfast four;

Redundant syllables of Summer rain,
  And displaced accents of authentic Spring:
Spondaic clouds above a gusty plain
  With dactyls on the wing. . . .

And the poem goes on, after a most happy metaphor to the effect that the laws of English verse are not "Common law, but equity," to compare the freedoms within English verse law to the comparatively narrower limits of the French and Italian systems.

Surely, a subject for a poem which suggests at first only the possibility of a *tour de force,* but the three stanzas just quoted show that even on such a subject Mrs. Meynell still speaks as a poet.

There are only 144 pages in the final collection of Mrs. Meynell's work, but so closely packed is her richness that every poem tempts one to extensive commentary. Indeed, had Meredith written some of them, extensive commentary would have been necessary, for most poems at once of thought and lyricism are likely to be obscure even with the best of auctorial intentions. But Mrs. Meynell will never need the sort of criticism we find in Trevelyan's interpretative book about Meredith's poetry. She can be at once thought-packed and crystalline clear. Intellectually she has always lived a most vigorously athletic life and gives the lie to the idea that intellectual sophistication is incompatible with the simple power to feel direct emotions. Indeed, it is the really sophisticated, the knowing, person who can by very wealth of association gain the greatest amount of emotional implication out of the simplest things. And the record of such a gain, such an exemplification of the fact that spiritually to him who hath shall be given, is found in the poem "A Thrush Before Dawn," the quotation of which will be the best close to these notes on a woman poet who is unique in her particular excellences and certainly among the immortals:

A voice peals in this end of night
    A phrase of notes resembling stars,
Single and spiritual notes of light,
    What call they at my window bars?
The South, the past, the day to be,
An ancient infelicity.

Darkling, deliberate, what sings
    This wonderful one, alone, at peace?
What wilder things than song, what things
    Sweeter than youth, clearer than Greece,
Dearer than Italy, untold
Delight, and freshness centuries old?

201

First Impressions

And first first-loves, a multitude,
   The exaltation of their pain;
Ancestral childhood long renewed:
   And midnights of invisible rain;
And gardens, gardens, night and day,
Gardens and childhood all the way.

What Middle Ages passionate,
O passionless voice! What distant bells
Lodged in the hills, what palace state
   Illyrian! For it speaks, it tells,
Without desire, without dismay,
Some morrow and some yesterday.

All-natural things! But more—Whence came
   This yet remoter mystery?
How do these starry notes proclaim
   A graver still divinity?
This hope, this sanctity of fear?
O innocent throat! O human ear!

Criticism in General

I

A FRIEND recently suggested that I should write (for the readers of my weekly literary review (in the first instance) one or two articles explaining the principles upon which criticism rested. The suggestion was a good one, for nowhere is our American mind more at sea than in questions of criticism—and questions of criticism are also questions of appreciation, for every reader who enjoys a book or fails to enjoy it and gives himself a reason is a critic. Criticism is a spiritual activity which takes place whenever one reacts consciously to a work of art. It may or may not be followed by the practical activity of putting one's critical reaction down upon paper.

It so happened that shortly after this suggestion was made, Mr. J. C. Squire first published his poem entitled "The Stockyards: Chicago," which has since been printed in his "American Poems" and which lends itself beautifully to purposes of demonstration.

Here is a piece of work in poetic form which is concrete, pictorial, and which is certainly moving; a record of something that moved Mr. Squire profoundly and that transmits his emotion to us. And yet it might well be argued whether this is a work of art at all, or whether it is something else entirely which has simply borrowed the clothing of a work of art.

What happened was this: Mr. Squire visited the stockyards and a number of things happened to him. He was filled with pity for the victims, for one thing, and, for another, he was made physically sick by the outward manner of their fate. And undoubtedly the one attitude was influenced by the other. Probably Mr. Squire accepts with a certain equanimity the fact that these animals would, in a state of nature, perish with more or less pain. And probably he would accept with equanimity the fact that we kill them in their prime if he knew that it was done in a painless manner—indeed, that would be preferable to their death by starvation or disease or the attacks of other animals in a state of nature.

But taking the thing as it is, what ought a man to do about it when he is affected as Mr. Squire was? He might say that the whole thing was so dirty and iniquitous that no decent man would have anything to do with it—and therewith become a vegetarian. Mr. Squire has not done that. Neither did Mr. Galsworthy, when he was similarly disgusted by conditions under which animals in England were killed. What he did do, however, was to write pamphlets and take other practical action toward reform in those methods—for it is well known that in Germany they use humane methods, and while it would have been disloyal to say this during the war, it may be safe to say so now without inviting any accusation of pro-Germanism.

Now Mr. Squire's poem will do either one of two things: It will merely sicken and depress its reader without further result, or it will cause him to agitate for reform in stockyard methods or to become a vegetarian. The first result is not desirable in itself, and the second result will be negligible for even though this poem has since been published in book form in America how many people in this country are in the habit of reading Mr. Squire's poetry?—or anyone else's for that matter.

What, then, has criticism to say of such a performance as this of Mr. Squire's? It might certainly begin by saying that this is a mixed performance. Mr. Squire mixes two subjects: our infliction of pain upon the lower creatures, and our infliction of death upon them—things which in practice are largely separable, and which, if the stockyard people did separate them, would leave his poem in bad shape even as a document. He mixes two or more sets of emotions—his tragic pity for beings condemned to death; his emotional and physical horror at the nasty accompaniments of that death, his satiric sense of the irrational gap between those physical horrors and the gaiety, good humor, blindness to the tragedy, of the people

205

who work in the yard—he has an effective picture of
the pretty girls who wrap the hams and chatter among
themselves without any apparent sense of the horrors
just a few rooms away—and of the other people who
live in Chicago and go to opera quite unconscious
of the inferno so near them. Now some of those
emotions are inherent in his theme; others, like his
physical nausea, are only incidental.

And again his results are mixed; we are so shocked
by the physical details of his theme that we do not
think at all of his art. Our reaction is all along
practical lines—practical, that is, in the wide sense
of the term; we may feel like becoming vegetarians
or like seeking for humaner methods in the stockyards. There is only one thing that we feel like doing
with the poem as apart from the things in it—and that
is, not read it again.

But when criticism has said all that about Mr.
Squire's work it has really condemned it as a work
of art. For a work of art has its own origin and
its own sphere and effects, and to drive the reader
to reformatory action is not its sphere and function,
for, if it were, every successful work of art would
effect some reform, and, the reform effected, the excuse
for and the facts embodied in, the work of art would
be gone, and the work would have done that which
was required of it and would cease to exist. But one
prime quality of works of art is that they interest
us permanently. The rise of feminism does not affect

Shakespeare's heroines. The abolition of war by the League of Nations would not put Homer in the discard—although it might make "Alice in Wonderland" look commonplace.

Then what is a work of art? It is simply the record, in whatever medium, of some particular perception. It is our first conversation with Mother Nature and Father Time before they have begun to teach us lessons, and also our heart-to-heart talks with them after the lessons have been learned. When Walter de la Mare, writing of "Noon and Night Flower," tells us that:

> Lovely beyond the rest
>   Are these of all delight—
> The tiny pimpernel that noon loves best,
>   The primrose palely burning through the night.
>
> One 'neath day's burning sky,
>   With ruby decks her place,
> The other when Eve's chariot glideth by
>   Lifts her dim torch to light that dreaming face.

—he is not telling us anything that we can compare to something else and from which we can announce a conclusion. He is only bringing us back to a simple recognition of something that we call beautiful because there mere perception puts us and Nature at our ease together—and we recognize in her ourselves. To talk of the "moral lesson" in such poetry is an impertinence in both the true and colloquial senses of the word.

First Impressions

And, on the other hand, in our sophisticated conversations, when all the lessons are learned, and when we read King Lear, we find ourselves in a region far and away beyond that of practical necessity, and beyond anything we "can do about it."

That, of course, is the truth behind the often-heard and misunderstood phrase "art for art's sake." Art for art's sake does not mean that art is more important than morals or is to be pursued to the exclusion of every other interest. It simply means that art is a region free and autonomous. It cannot be bent to ends of moral edification or practical propaganda without coarsening, warping and cheapening it, any more than a church steeple can be turned into a silo. And even the most practical farmer would hardly dare to suggest that the church trustee ask the architect to plan a church without a steeple, on the ground that it served no practical purpose. Yet the average American always asks for the "moral" of a work of art, and I have no doubt that the Vegetarian Societies of America have already written to Mr. Squire, asking his permission to reprint his stockyard poem for propaganda—and that is a reason why I do not think that it is a work of art.

This does not mean that I do not sympathize with Mr. Squire's feelings, because I do. But when—and here is the ultimate test—his poem comes into our consciousness, it pulls that consciousness in various

ways—as I have already outlined. When a real work
of art comes into the consciousness it unifies it, there
is a total impression, as there is in King Lear as
well as in the shortest lyric. And the same material
may give either the cross-pull of conflicting emotions,
ideas, purposes, as Mr. Squire has done in this poem,
or, properly used, it may give us an artistic impression.
Indeed Shakespeare has given us in a very short poem
all that is aesthetic in Mr. Squire's long one, and here
it is:

> Why, let the stricken deer go weep,
>   The hart ungallèd play;
> For some must watch, while some must sleep
>   So runs the world away.

the parallelism, applying, of course, only to the
first two lines.

For there is Mr. Squire's pitying version without his
nausea; the antinomies of his poem without its con-
tingencies and accidentals.

II

I have said that a work of art should give one a
unified impression—an impression in which the spirit
can rest, a sense of achievement. It ought not to
arouse merely one's practical interests. Anyone who
has read Croce's "Aesthetic" can give the theoretical

reasons for this, and anyone, however innocent of philosophy, who has really experienced works of art, knows that it is true.

But there is always more than one way of stating a truth, and one of the best statements of this truth not involving philosophical terms, is that of an English psychologist, who tells us that impressions of beauty rest upon "psychical distance." It is well known, by now, that beauty is not an objective property of bodies or even of nature. Beauty is not only relative but its abiding place is in the human spirit and not in the outside world. Physical objects or imaginative representations mediate beauty to us under certain conditions, and the prime condition is "psychic distance." A single example will show what is meant. Shakespeare's song:

> Full fathom five thy father lies,
> Of his bones are coral made;
> Those are pearls that were his eyes,
> Nothing of him that doth fade
> But doth suffer a sea change. . . .

—is undoubtedly beautiful because although the physical imagery of which it is made up has all to do with drowning, we are not, as we read it, brought psychically near to the idea of drowning. If we happened to hear that song just after we had been rescued from drowning, we should have lost that psychic distance, the thing would come too near home and would sound—and for us would validly be—a horrible and macabre burlesque. It is because the poem does come too close home, that Squire's "Stockyard: Chicago" is not a work of art. To that poem nobody can take the requisite attitude of psychic distance. The same thing explains why people in general like books with happy endings and do not like tragedy. People in general do not achieve psychic distance easily: they far oftener identify their practical selves with the characters, and so a tragedy in which sympathetic characters die in the last act does not appeal to them. Of course the thing varies. For myself, Morris's poem, "The Haystack in the Rain," is doubtful. The agony is piled on just a little too thick for me to achieve the necessary distance. For some one with a tougher psychic hide the poem might come off successfully as a poem.

This principle throws light on the perennial American quarrel between the lover of art and the censor. The censor is an elected, appointed or self-chosen representative of the public at large, and reflects the public's attitude. Psychic distance is something of which he knows absolutely nothing. Even if he has never heard of Aristotle, he agrees with him that art is representation, although he thinks that it is literal representation, conditioned only by the fact that a man is not as accurate as a camera. And so this gentleman objects when Miss Anderson prints parts of James

First Impressions

Joyce's "Ulysses" in the *Little Review*. Lately James Joyce completed his "Ulysses" in an immense volume of about nine hundred closely printed pages, in a style which demands thought and application on the part of the reader. It is a story of the conscious lives, the reflections, the broken and rambling thoughts of certain people in Dublin; and the minuteness with which their inner lives are recorded is apparent when we learn that these nine hundred pages only cover the events of twenty-four hours. It is said that in this book James Joyce has invented a wholly new way in which to write fiction, has developed a fictional technique which is in line with the technique of the new psychology associated with Freud. Such critics as Ernest Boyd in this country and J. Middleton Murry in London, to say nothing of French critics, have taken the work very seriously. But we in America will not be able just yet to make up our minds whether Joyce has done all that is claimed for him or whether he has not. For the postoffice censors will not let his book into the country. If you ordered one from the publishers in Europe your copy would be confiscated, and you might even find yourself in the hands of a judge and jury. Why?

Because Joyce, in trying to present to us the total thoughts of two human beings—a man and a woman —has had to include their thoughts and feelings on sex. Joyce himself is not trying to make these people heroic or attractive; indeed, he is exhibiting them as vulgar and commonplace. And so he does not "play up" their sex life and make it sound attractive. Indeed, Ernest Boyd, writing in the New York *Tribune,* says that Joyce represents the sex side of these people's lives in somewhat the spirit of the mediaeval church. Certainly nobody reading the book would be led into temptation or even be led to think of the beauty of sex—it is the ugliness and unpleasantness of it that would strike him.

Then why is the book suppressed? Simply because the censor cannot imagine for a moment a human being who is detached enough to read that book and look at the thing as a whole, with the sex part in its due place. And so serious American students of literature are to be denied the chance to study a piece of literature which all Europe is discussing, and it is made worth while, at the same time, for smugglers of erotic literature to add one more to the books for which they can get high prices simply because they are forbidden.

Such a thing would not be possible if we had an informed and active public opinion which could discriminate between what was art and what was not. But we have no such body of opinion and meanwhile we are at the mercy of these ignorant masters who tell us what we shall or shall not read—but who can only enforce their decrees on that part of our population which does not have $50 to spend—those who have that amount being able to get Mr. Joyce's book through some underground channel.

First Impressions

So far I have told, for the most part, what a work of art is not—and that is a less difficult thing than to tell what it is. Indeed, Rupert Brooke, in his book on John Webster, went so far as to say there was no common principle uniting the arts, that there was nothing to be inferred from the facts of, say, our reactions to painting, that would help us in formulating a theory of what constituted art in poetry. But the arts do have things in common; for instance, in every form of art we have rhythm, and the things that are common to them all might suggest that there was a psychology common to them all.

One explanation of the arts is that they delight us by the fact that they have form. A picture is good because its composition and something deeper than composition—organization of masses—is good, that and not because its mere "subject" is interesting. A poem is good because it has "form." Indeed, we have seen an adherent of this idea praise a novel by George Moore because its form suggested that of a symphony. Obviously this explanation of the arts would appeal especially to a musician.

But it happens that the most consistent application of the theory was made by the English art critic, Clive Bell, in his little book, "Art." And Mr. Bell has more recently written another book, "Since Cezanne." It is interesting to compare the two books.

214

First Impressions

In his first book Mr. Bell argued that since a picture
gave us aesthetic pleasure and a design in arabesque
or a simple vase gave us aesthetic pleasure, the quality
that made each a work of art must be something that
was common to them both. So that if the picture
represented a cow its aesthetic worth could not lie in
the fact that we thought the cow was a nice cow—for
in that event what did we recognize in the arabesque
that made it pleasing to us? No, he said, what moves
us in the vase, the arabesque, the picture of a cow, the
cathedral or a piece of music, is not a resemblance to
anything we know in life—it is simply "form" or, as
he put it, "significant form," for everything has a form
but few forms are aesthetically moving. By form Mr.
Bell did not merely mean pattern or composition, but
something deeper—he was not quite clear himself as
to what it was, but he was sure that it was significant
not because it represented an object but whether it did
or not. This was a good theory in one way—it enabled
him to accept both modern non-representative painting
and primitive painting and to explain the charm of
African sculpture. But it was a bad theory for this
reason—literature, even lyrical poetry, can never be
pure form, purged from all recognition of objects. A
lyric must always be about something—and so Mr.
Bell had to tell us that literature was an impure form
of art, that from it only a diluted and adulterated
aesthetic pleasure could be obtained. Only to the
painter, the sculptor and to the musician (although

215

for his own part, he admitted, he did not always "get" musical form) was the real, genuine, and only beatific vision allowed.

And if form did not signify any section of life, of what was it significant? Ah, said Mr. Bell, there we come to mysticism—perhaps significant form reveals to us otherwise hidden realities in the universe.

Well, that was rather tough on us people who get more from literature than from painting—or who get as much. And so it is interesting to see that in Mr. Bell's later volume, "Since Cezanne," he is not quite so sure of his aesthetic form. He condescends to write of Renoir not only as a painter but as a reflector of French life and character. And he writes about absolute beauty as if he were in grave doubt whether such a thing existed. His first article, "Since Cezanne," shows him definitely against any merely doctrinaire development—such as strict cubism—and that and other essays reveal that he looks for a revival of traditionalism in painting—especially in French painting.

Mr. Bell has much to say of criticism in general in this volume, and he makes some very good points. One of them—in answer to the often petulant attitude of artists and authors toward critics—is that the critic does not exist for the sake of the artist but for the sake of the public. That is true. Another is that a critic of a representative art—poetry, the novel, the drama —ought to serve an apprenticeship writing of the nonrepresentative arts. For then he would be forced to express aesthetic judgments and would not take the easy way of writing about the moral side or the anecdotal side of literary art.

But, to come back to our main question, if Mr. Bell's hypothesis of "significant form" seems to land us nowhere except possibly in mysticism, what is the truth of the matter? We may let a detailed answer to that go over, merely saying now that all that is true in Mr. Bell's idea is to be found in Benedetto Croce's theory of art as expression. For the moment, and using a term that Croce does not use because he analyzes it into more fundamental concepts, we may say that art is the expression of emotion.

It would be more accurate to say that art is the expression of some intuition and that that is always accompanied by emotion. And by expression is not meant a mere denoting. There is a picture in the Chicago Art Institute which denotes or represents a battle scene—lots of blood, wounded men and horses, etc. But a well-known art critic once assured me that it was the most peaceful picture he had ever seen. For its forms, taken as pure form, harmonized in such a way, and its colors were so quiet and so balanced that, to anyone who could forget the subject, the effect of the painting as such was one of quietness and delightful calm. I do not vouch for the criticism, but such a thing is certainly possible. It would simply mean that while the artist as a conscious man was trying to paint a battle scene, the unconscious artist in

217

him got the upper hand and expressed something entirely different.

IV

I could not better conclude these remarks on criticism than by some comment on and quotation from the one book that, more than any other, has influenced contemporary thinking upon the subject. That book is "Aesthetic," by Benedetto Croce; translated by Douglas Ainslie and recently issued in a new edition with the historical section now completely translated for the first time.

The subtitle of this book: "As Science of Expression and General Linguistic," may scare a few readers away for it sounds rather forbidding, and indeed the book is a rather technical one, not to be completely grasped at one reading. But even the reader who does not know much about philosophy will find in the book not only technical philosophy but wisdom, and our quotations shall be from the less technical passages.

Croce's coupling of aesthetics and linguistics simply means that in his view language is an expressive function, that its words primarily express intuitions: that language is perpetual creation, and an artificial or universal language a mere chimera. But our present concern is with art. Art, says Croce, is the expression of an intuition, but by intuition he does not mean anything mystical or magical or even Bergsonian. He begins his book thus:

218

First Impressions

Knowledge has two forms: it is either intuitive knowledge or logical knowledge; knowledge obtained through the imagination or knowledge obtained through the intellect; knowledge of the individual or knowledge of the universal; of individual things or of the relations between them: it is in fact, productive either of images or of concepts.

And the artist is not a freak or a man with a faculty which others have not:

The intuition of the simplest popular love-song, which says the same thing, or very nearly, as any declaration of love that issues at every moment from the lips of thousands of ordinary men, may be intensively perfect in its poor simplicity, though it be extensively so much more limited than the complex intuition of a love song by Leopardi.

The whole difference, then, is quantitative, and as such is indifferent to philosophy, scientia qualitatem. Certain men have a greater aptitude, a more frequent inclination fully to express certain complex states of the soul. These men are known in ordinary language as artists. Some very complicated and difficult expressions are not often achieved, and these are called works of art. The limits of the expression-intuitions that are called art, as opposed to those that are vulgarly called non-art, are empirical and impossible to define. If an epigram be art, why not a single word?

What, then, is the type of artist whom we call a genius? Croce answers:

Nor can we admit that the word genius or artistic genius, as distinct from the non-genius of the ordinary man, pos-

219

sesses more than a quantitative significance. Great artists are said to reveal us to ourselves. But how could this be possible, unless there were identity of nature between their imagination and ours, and unless the difference were only one of quantity. It were better to change "poeta nascitur" into "homo nascitur poeta": some men are born great poets, some small. The cult of the genius with all its attendant superstitions has arisen from this quantitative difference having been taken as a difference of quality. It has been forgotten that genius is not something that has fallen from heaven, but humanity itself. The man of genius who poses or is represented as remote from humanity finds his punishment in becoming or appearing somewhat ridiculous. Examples of this are the genius of the romantic period and the superman of our own time.

It might be said, indeed, that sanity is the keynote of Croce's aesthetic. But your ordinary person often confounds sanity with prosiness. Such people are themselves concerned only with the prose of life, and they tolerate the artist only so long as he stays within the bounds of what they consider proper—and even then only so far as he constitutes himself a sort of missionary for those interests. I heard, for instance, a lady at a recent "literary lunch" say, concerning the work of such Middle West writers as Sherwood Anderson and Theodore Dreiser—whose work she did not like—"if they are clever enough to write about the sordid and unpleasant they are clever enough to write about the beautiful if we insist upon it."

First Impressions

Unfortunately, it is not a matter of cleverness at all. There is a way to aid these men to write more cheerfully, and Croce tells us how it may be found. Whether this lady would be willing to do very much along the line Croce suggests, I do not know:

The true artist in fact, finds himself big with his theme, he knows not how; he feels the moment of birth drawing near, but he cannot will it or not will it. If he were to act in opposition to his inspiration, to make an arbitrary choice, if, born Anacreon, he should wish to sing of Atreus and of Alcides, his lyre would warn him of his mistake, sounding only of Venus and of Love, notwithstanding his efforts to the contrary. . . .

. . . And when the same critics object to the theme or content of works which they proclaim to be artistically perfect as being unworthy of art and blameworthy; if these expressions really are perfect, there is nothing to be done but to advise the critics to leave the artists in peace, for they can only derive inspiration from what has moved their soul. They should rather (the critics, that is) direct their attention toward effecting changes in surrounding nature and society; that such impressions and states of soul should not recur. If ugliness were to vanish from the world, if universal virtue and felicity were established there, perhaps artists would no longer represent perverse or pessimistic feelings, but calm, innocent, and joyous feelings, Arcadians of a real Arcady. But so long as ugliness and turpitude exist in nature and impose themselves upon the artist, to prevent the expression of these things also is impossible; and when it has arisen, "factum infectum fieri nequit."

First Impressions

And this leads us to the truth that art is independent of morals and of science and of the useful, and therefore, Croce indorses, when it is rightly understood, the idea of art for art's sake, or as he prefers to express it, the independence of art. Art does not even have the task, which many people who are above the more vulgar forms of error we have noted assign to it, of representing "the universal in the particular" or "the type in the individual," for an intuition cannot be of the general, and in the completed expression, say, of Don Quixote, Croce points out that the figure cannot represent all self-blinded men, because many self-blinded men are not by any means Don Quixotes: "Don Quixote is a type; but of what is he a type save of all Don Quixotes? A type, so to speak, of himself." And he goes on to say that we think of him as a universal type simply because "we find our own impressions fully determined and realized in the expression of a poet (for example in a poetical personage). We call that expression typical, which we might call simply aesthetic."

And Croce does away, too, with the notion of progress in art in the sense that there is progress in science:

... art is intuition, and intuition is individuality, and individuality does not repeat itself. ... At the most ... it may be asserted that the history of aesthetic productions shows progressive cycles, but each cycle with its own problem and each progressive only in respect to that problem. . . . Not only is the art of savages not inferior, as art, to that of civilized peoples, if it be correlative to the impressions of the savage . . . but none of these worlds can be compared to any other in respect of artistic value. . . .

Some, for instance, talk of the infancy of Italian art in Giotto, and of its maturity in Raphael or in Titian; as though Giotto were not complete and absolutely perfect, granted the material of feeling with which his mind was furnished. He was certainly incapable of drawing a figure like Raphael, or of coloring it like Titian; but was Raphael or Titian capable of creating the "Marriage of St. Francis with Poverty" or the "Death of St. Francis"? The spirit of Giotto had not felt the attraction of the body beautiful which the Renaissance studied and raised to a place of honor; the spirits of Raphael and of Titian were no longer interested in certain movements of ardor and of tenderness with which the man of the fourteenth century was in love. How, then, can a comparison be made, where there is no comparative term?

These quotations from Croce do not, of course, give us the basis of his philosophy—for that the reader must be referred to the book—but they do show us how essentially simple the question of aesthetics is when it is treated philosophically and without superstition and prejudice, and perhaps, even in translation and in their brevity, they show us that Croce himself is a literary artist and not a mere pedant.

The Periphery of Poetry

A MINOR example of the lack of taste and of justice with which the universe is conducted—the lack of poetic justice in it, in fact—is that poetry can actually be written by ignorant people and even by mad people —no, not William Blake but Christopher Smart and John Clare—while the wisest and most painstaking scholars can not even tell us what poetry is. They are justified, however, in writing books about poetry, for there are a great many things that poetry is often taken for, and is not. What may look like pedantry is amply justified when its aim is to clear away the real pedantry of the days when poetry had to be morally edifying and its structure artificially scannable.

Certainly this has been the real value of the many recent books written on the general subject of poetics. As a rule, these books have abandoned the pretentiousness of their forbears: they have quoted Aristotle less and less; and, indeed, have largely transferred their attention from his forms of poetry to the lyric. The student of the subject who goes no further back than the Oxford Lectures on Poetry by Professor A. C. Bradley and Professor J. W. Mackail—two recent incumbents of that unique university-chair which is occupied by a new man every five years—and follows them up with Sir Henry Newbolt's "A New Study of English Poetry," Mr. John Livingstone Lowes's "Convention and Revolt in Poetry" and Professor Bliss Perry's new "Study of Poetry," will have his apprehension of poetry in general quickened, and will be fully able to steer himself among the rival camps of traditional and schismatic versifiers and polyphonic prosers.

Of these books Professor Perry's is, perhaps, the most comprehensive; but it pays the penalty for this by being the most peripheral. It is avowedly written with the classroom's needs in view, as well as those of the inquiring general reader; and the former aim to some extent vitiates the author's treatment by imposing too eclectic an ideal upon him. The book is a *résumé* of poetics rather than a personal confession; and the heart of the matter can only be reached when a schooled thinker, Sir Henry Newbolt, for a shining example, uses aesthetic theory simply to illuminate his own personal experience.

For a book written on the lines mentioned, this is, however, surprisingly open-minded. By his discussion of the mechanism through which poetry "gets across," Professor Perry shows any poets of the Bodenheim wing of insurgency how futile it is for them to write such lines as "the colour of the birth of a white throat," which is not quoted by Professor Perry but is taken from an early number of the *Little Review*. That line was doubtless perfectly good poetry to its creator, but it lacks what Professor Perry

225

calls "transmission-value." "If words were merely representations of private experience," Mr. Perry says,° "merely our nicknames for things, they would not pass the walls of the garden inhabited by each man's imagination. 'Expression' would be possible, but 'communication' would be impossible."

The factors which make for transmission-value are brilliantly discussed in this book; although occasionally the author leaves antinomies open. For instance, he quotes Poe and Edmond Holmes to the effect that as poetry deals in vague emotions, its words should also be vague: "words of large import and with many meanings or shades of meaning. Precision . . . is always unpoetical." And then he quotes the Imagistic dictum concerning "hardness and economy of speech; the exact word," dropping the subject without attempting the perfectly easy reconciliation. For effective poetry is the fruit of the most rigorous word-selection, to the end that the impression shall be conveyed with micrometric exactness, while the impression itself is something that surrounds the hard core of the thing denoted by an umbral fringe of suggestiveness.

This cardinal point in poetics has been brilliantly worked out by Mr. Arthur Ransome in an article on "Kinetic and Potential Speech" in his "Portraits and Speculations":

Energy [says Mr. Ransome] is described by physicists as kinetic and potential. Kinetic energy is force actually exerted. Potential energy is force that a body is in a position to exert. Applying these two terms to language, without attempting too strict an analogy, I wish to define literature, or rather the medium of literature, as a combination of kinetic with potential speech. In this combination the two are coincident. There is no such thing in literature as speech purely kinetic or purely potential. Purely kinetic speech is prose, not good prose, not literature, but colourless prose, prose without atmosphere, the sort of prose that M. Jourdain discovered he had been speaking all his life. It says things. An example of purely potential speech may be found in music. I do not think it can be made with words, though we can give our minds a taste of it in listening to a meaningless but narcotic incantation, or a poem in a language that we do not understand.

Then, after quoting Blake's

> Tiger! Tiger! burning bright
> In the forests of the night
> What immortal hand or eye
> Could frame thy fearful symmetry—

Mr. Ransome points out its potential as well as kinetic aspects:

It is impossible to deny the power of suggestion wielded by those four lines, a power utterly disproportionate to what is actually said. The kinetic base of that stanza is only the proposition to a supposed tiger of a difficult problem in metaphysics. But above, below, and on either side of that question, completely enveloping it, is the phosphorescence

227

of another speech, that we can not so easily overhear. And who shall speak in fit terms of its potentiality? That glowing image, that surprised address; not in enumeration of such things shall we come upon its secret.

In that passage, the critic is pointing from the periphery of poetry toward its nucleus; and it is a pity that in a bibliography and list of references which reaches all the way from Aristotle to the egregious "Science of Poetry" of Mr. Hiram Maxim, Professor Perry has overlooked Mr. Ransome's brilliant essay.

Mr. Ransome's sentences also suggest another phase of poetry in which most critics, including the present one, face the circumference instead of the centre. He tells us that nonsense-verses appeal because they are, to a certain extent and at least unimpededly, potential. Professor Perry, on the other hand, with the usual prejudice of scholars against decoration in art and poetry, thinks that nonsense-verses are decorative poetry carried to an extreme:

Nevertheless, though absolutely pure decorative beauty does not exist, the artist may push the decorative principle very far, so far indeed, that his product lacks interest and proves tedious or nonsensical. There is nonsense-verse, as we shall see later, which fulfils every condition for pure formal beauty in poetry. Yet it is not poetry but only nonsense-verse.

That is a mischievous libel on all decorative art. It would certainly rule most music out of court.

228

First Impressions

Nonsense-verse is essentially anarchistic, and decorative art is essentially law-abiding. The question is, what does decoration mean in poetry? "Kubla Khan" is certainly decorative poetry if there ever were any; and yet its emotional effect is so great, so constant, and so widely attested that we can not dismiss it as nonsense. Mr. Walter de la Mare's "The Listeners" is decorative and most moving. Or take that very beautiful poem of Mr. de la Mare's that begins:

> There was nought in the Valley
> But a Tower of Ivory,
> Its base enwreathed with red
> Flowers that at evening
> Caught the sun's crimson
> As to Ocean low he sped—

and then carries us on through a series of beautifully pictured changes until:

> And on high in its lantern
> A shape of the living
> Watched o'er a shoreless sea,
> From a Tower rotting,
> With age and weakness,
> Once lovely as ivory.

The title of this poem is "Time Passes" and to that extent the poem has an intellectual meaning and so, it may be objected, it is not purely decorative. But the

229

intellectual meaning is only the kinetic aspect. Why does the decorative treatment do so much more? By what magic does it disturb us? In that question is the hidden heart of the whole matter—the heart that all these critics of poetry in general tend to ignore. Are they afraid of the mysticism that is implied in any attempt at an answer? Would it be too uncritical a hypothesis to say that, just as the patent onomatopœia of such descriptive poetry as Bridges's "London Snow" with its flakes "Stealthily and perpetually falling and loosely lying" moves us by its power of re-creation, so in these poems to which we can attach no definite intellectual meaning that is on a parity with their emotional power, there may be an onomatopœic rendering of realities, of perhaps a beyond that is within us, that can in no other way be attained?

But to regard poetry so, is only to make more important than ever the questions of its technique and materials that concern alike the poet who would avoid slovenly workmanship and the reader who would read with ear attuned as well as mind. And these questions Professor Perry has handled with a catholicity rare among American academic critics.

Free Verse and its Propaganda

POETRY is written by ear and is recognized by the ear, and only when it obeys the laws of rhythm do we recognize it as poetry. But just as knowledge of law is indispensable to any man who contemplates either breaking it or "sailing close to the wind" and of very little use to the man who is naturally decent and owns his own home, so knowledge of the principles of metrics is indispensable to the metrical innovator and not of much use to the poet who sings out of a full inspiration as well as out of a traditional background.

Whether one likes free verse or not is largely a matter of taste. The real question is whether one likes what has been done in free verse. To say that the medium itself is good or bad is rather silly, for, after all, free verse is simply language written in cadence—or as Dr. Patterson, of Columbia University, has more or less proved—it is prose with the rhythm emphasized by the line structure; and nobody likes or dislikes prose as such. Our like or dislike is for Conrad, or Meredith, or W. H. Hudson, or Dr. Frank Crane.

Perhaps the salient thing about the free verse movement, however, is not its actual achievement (for what free verse writer of our time is either more realistic

231

than Wilfrid Wilson Gibson or, in certain moods, Mr. Hardy or Mr. Lawrence, all on the one hand, or more mystical and suggestive than Walter de la Mare, on the other hand? Or more psycho-analytical than Mr. Lawrence or Mr. T. S. Eliot—who generally use metre and rhyme?), but it is the intense propaganda promoted by the free verse writers for their particular methods. There are even examples of free verse writers and imagists reviewing their own work under aliases or anonymously, but I do not mean that. I mean the more dignified propaganda of the essay on the technique of poetry. Practically all of these essays seek to give metreless verse prestige by the utterly false statement that metred verse is an artificial thing whose possible combinations and permutations have already been exhausted. Young poets who have not studied metrics may read these articles, take their assertions for truth, and turn away from what are really their best possibilities. The writer knows of one particular case, that of a young free verse writer who is very well known among his "schoolfellows," whose work has appeared in more than one magazine and who has won a considerable prize for his poetry. He happens to have had little formal education in English, and to have read radical verse and criticism almost exclusively. In one of his poems occur these lines:—

> Let no blasphemer till the sacred earth
> Or scatter seed upon it. . . .

232

First Impressions

The writer remarked to him that he had achieved a rather good line and a half of iambic pentameter.

"What's that?" asked the puzzled poet, who had been led to believe by sundry articles in *Poetry* that iambic pentameter was a "strait-waistcoat," but had come no nearer than that to finding out what it really was.

Obviously these propagandist-metricians may do damage, so that it seems worth while to examine one of their pronouncements. In *The Musical Quarterly* for January, 1920, Miss Amy Lowell has a very interesting article on "Some Musical Analogies in Modern Poetry." Her main theme is the likenesses she hears between the free rhythms of what she calls modern verse—that is to say, free verse (from a more traditional point of view blank verse has "free" rhythms)—and the music of such men as Debussy, Scriabine, and their *confrères*. The analogies she points out are doubtless valid, and her paper is very suggestive. But the ignorance of the basis of English verse which it displays is so astounding that one can only imagine that a prejudice against that form of writing has in some way clouded Miss Lowell's vision and memory. Were ordinary English verse what she says as it is, it were well indeed to abandon it.

And the curious thing is that Miss Monroe, writing in *Poetry*, says very nearly the same thing, although she hides her quite unmodern conception of verse rhythm under the mantle of Sidney Lanier's theories, while from internal evidence we should judge that Miss Lowell has read no metrician later than Poe, whose "Rationale of English Verse" left much to be desired as a systematic treatise.

The first of Miss Lowell's strictures on our regular verse concerns the monotony of Alexander Pope—a charge that may well be granted, except that she remarks that the verse of his period was even more monotonous than the music of the time, because "the system of rests employed in music gave some variation of effect within the pattern, whereas the verses sounded monotonously on every beat with never an omission. . . ."

Now that is not accurate, as there were phrase-pauses in Pope, and even in the most orthodox blank verse there is a delicate syncopation due to the pauses between words, pauses which are often not recognized —so that metricians have said that our iambic verse is in three-eight time because the syllables of each foot are equivalent to three shorts, whereas more careful metricians, notably Mr. Omond, declare that the pauses between words, if taken as metrical rests, make our blank verse duple, a very different thing from triple time.

But worse follows. Miss Lowell, who begins her article with a fling at the "smart ignorance" of those who venture to criticize her, has apparently neither heard of Lanier nor read Saintsbury. She does quote Poe in this essay, and from her total ignorance of the fact that there is a recognized metrical pause in verse structure, something which Poe also conspicuously overlooked, one is led to believe that he is her main authority in these matters. But here is Miss Lowell's own statement of the metrical foundation of our regular verse:—

We speak of metrical verse because it is a verse based on metre. The unit of metre is the foot, and a metrical line contains a given number of such feet, what number being determined beforehand by the pattern chosen for the whole poem. There are only five feet proper to English metre: the iambus, the trochee, the anapæst, the dactyl, and the spondee. Some metrists even deny the existence of the latter [*sic*]. Any attempt to foist the use of other feet into the analysis defeats itself, since all longer feet are capable of being split up into one or other of the main four I have given, and of course a unit must be the lowest possible element into which anything can be divided. It is surprising what a number of changes the poets have been able to ring out of this seemingly inflexible medium. But, even so, there are many rhythms that they simply could not render. The terrible defect of no rests was an insurmountable handicap. . . .

Taking the last point first, we may imagine with what trouble Mother Goose managed to overcome that handicap of no rests. But she did it, as this quotation testifies:—

> Pease porridge hot, pease porridge cold,
> Pease porridge in the pot, nine days old.

235

First Impressions

Any child who recites that instinctively catches the good Mother's intention, and children have never had any difficulty in unconsciously "scanning" the lines—their reading was their scansion.

Mother Goose having showed him how to do it, Browning was also able to overcome this terrible handicap:—

> Kentish Sir Byng stood for his king,
> Bidding the crop-headed parliament swing.

The rest after "Byng" is very obviously of the same time-value as the syllables "headed," and it is a truly metrical rest; that is to say, it is not a mere grammatical pause, but has its exact musical or mathematical relation to the time-structure of the line.

Even so orthodox a metrician as Saintsbury allows for the rest in the scansion of regular verse, and Lanier has gone into the matter in great detail. But Miss Lowell has apparently never heard that a whole system of scansion for verse on musical analogies has been worked out, and that her iambics and dactyls and doubtful spondees wear a rather faded look to-day. Certainly, they are used only analogically, for an English "accentual iambic" may be in quantity-arrangement a classical trochee, a spondee, or almost what you will,—very often a pyrrhic. Certainly, if English verse has iambics in the accentual sense it also has spondees. Poe, we believe, ruled them out (another straw pointing to the source of Miss Lowell's

236

metrics), but as long as we write verse with two level stresses or with two long syllables coming together we have spondees. For instance, consider passages from more than one of Shakespeare's sonnets:—

Sap checkt with frost and lustie leaves quite gone.

or—

Makes black night beauteous, and her old face new.

But Miss Lowell's treatment of the pentameter line is based purely on the foregoing artificial considerations. She does not criticize the actual work of the poets—even when she compliments them on what they have been able to "wring out" of this inflexible medium. Had Miss Lowell gone to the original poems, instead of to a very doubtful theory of their structure, she would have known that the real poets did not wring out changes on a fixed framework at all. They wrote by ear, being guided by a very loose convention, and their scansion was either an afterthought or else they never scanned at all. Miss Lowell says that a line of Keats has "an even more daring innovation" than the displacing of an accent, for in—

Young companies nimbly began dancing

"one accent is deliberately suppressed and the next boldly displaced, to be followed by only one true accent, and to end on another displacement." Miss

237

First Impressions

Lowell is greatly surprised at what she calls the suppression and displacement of accents, whereas it is quite a matter of course in nearly all blank verse. And again, she tells us that a line of Robert Frost's has three accents, "where a blank verse line should have five."

As a matter of fact, however, a blank verse line should not have five "undisplaced" accents, and it need not have five at all. Shakespeare, for instance, writes:—

I do remember an apothecary.

The most that we can really say of a blank verse line is that it shall have ten syllables, with a tendency to alternate stress; or that duple rising metre is its norm. But we must always remember that if blank verse keeps to its norm it is, as Robert Bridges says, "more likely to madden than to lull." How "bold" Keats is in suppressing an accent we may imagine when we remember that Milton's "Paradise Lost" begins with a very irregular line and moves through twenty-six lines before reaching one regular blank verse line:—

And justify the ways of God to men.

When we remember that as many as three of the five feet of a blank verse line may be trisyllabic, we see how essentially different blank verse is from the

strait and narrow thing that Miss Lowell holds up
to terrify young poets.

In fact, blank verse is even a freer medium than
is sometimes implied when we say that the syllables
may be increased in any line to thirteen or so by the
use of trisyllabic feet, and that its accents may be
displaced or occluded. It is so free that often the
problem is to avoid writing it when one wishes to
write prose. It is so free, indeed, that it really evades
scansion altogether. Recent discussion amply attests
this. If blank verse were actually in three-eight
time—as Lanier asserts—"Paradise Lost" would be
slightly more suggestive of a waltz than it is. But
while our lyric measures have their rhythm set for
them by beats occurring at isochronous intervals, the
"feet" of blank verse do not do this at all. From
one to three of the beats may be quite theoretical.
The line may begin with a trochee instead of an
iambic foot. The isochronous intervals which some
prosodists have asserted to be there are unheard by
others. In a recent discussion in the London *Times*,
T. Sturge Moore, a poet of achievement and a scholar,
took issue with Dr. D. S. MacColl on this very matter, and the resulting correspondence showed an utter
lack of agreement on the subject. T. B. Rudmose-
Brown, the late Thomas MacDonagh, and Robert
Bridges, though not agreeing in anything else, all agree
in making syllabic verse of this variety a *genre* in
itself. In this type of verse, says MacDonagh in

the little book, "Thomas Campion and the Art of English Poetry," the only isochronous interval is the line. The line is "weighted" by long syllables following short, by accented syllables following unaccented—which is not of course the same thing—and by syllables of differing pitch. The throwing of the phrase across from one line to the next gives a further variation. Obviously, any attempt to scan mechanically such a line is hopeless.

On the other hand, what MacDonagh calls "song verse," including lyric measures and the measures which Bridges would call "stress verse," is determined by beats occurring at equal time-intervals. We have usually called such verse by classical names, but the names are really meaningless. Miss Lowell gives us a beautiful example of how meaningless they are. She tells us that in a poem, "After Hearing a Waltz by Bartok,—"

I attempted to reproduce waltz rhythm, a perfectly regular thing and one which it might be supposed quite possible to render in strict metre. Horror of horrors! it was not. The dactylic metre I had proposed to myself gave no swing in words, and I was obliged to fall back upon the bastard waltz accent of the anapæstic.

Fortunately, Miss Lowell was not obliged to fall far, because in any sequence of more than one or two feet the two measures are the same. If the reader doubt it let him look up Charles Kingsley's "Andromeda." Kingsley meant to write it in accentual hexameters, a dactylic metre. But it reads in anapæsts, and as anapæstic Saintsbury scans it. It is simply a matter of the convenience of beginning the foot with the accented or with the unaccented syllable. In fact, some metricians scan all English verse dactylically or trochaically, always beginning the foot with the accented syllable, and if a line begins with an unaccented syllable—as any typically iambic or anapæstic line would—they simply mark off the initial unaccented syllable or syllables and call it an anacrusis, or, if they are very consistent musical scansionists, they call it the remainder of the bar begun by the last accented syllable in the line above. For instance, one of the lines in Miss Lowell's poem reads:—

I was drunk with the lust of his life.

This may be divided anapæstically:—

I was drunk | with the lust | of his life,

or, dactylically with anacrusis:—

I was | drunk with the | lust of his | life,

in which latter case "life" is an incomplete foot to be completed by the anacrusis of the next line.

Most of us, however, will not care for this way of dividing verse, since it breaks up the metric unity of the line, but it is theoretically sound. And, inci-

241

dentally, it may be said that if we desire to speak of
feet in English verse as Miss Lowell does, we should
be more systematic in our use of foot terms.   Many
an anapæst in English does not consist of two short
syllables followed by a long; nor of two short syllables
unaccented, followed by an accented syllable; but of
a short and a long syllable, followed by another long
with or without a slight accent on it.   For instance,
let the reader observe these lines from James Joyce:—

> The grey winds, the cold winds are blowing
>   Where I go.

Now, of all the feet that Miss Lowell gives us for
English verse, the only one that will fit that first line
is the anapæst, so that the line would scan thus:—

> The grey winds, | the cold winds | are blow | ing—

—two anapæsts, an iambic, and a hypermetrical ending,—so-called.   But really those two anapæsts are
each what a Greek metrician would call a bacchius,
and if we use the one term, why not the other?   For
they do not give the same rhythmic effect as ordinary
anapæsts.   But this quotation may illustrate another
error in Miss Lowell's metrics.   She informs us of a
sample of free verse that she quotes, which changes
its rhythm at the end, that "the change of movement
at the end is something which the older poetry had
no means of achieving except by an abrupt jump to

another metre. Such a jump would have been far too violent . . . ," etc.

Now that statement is quite out of accord with the facts. We have seen a line—that quoted above—which, if we keep to Miss Lowell's terminology, has to be called predominantly anapæstic. But some readers have already objected to that scansion of the line on the ground that in point of fact it is a purely amphibrachic line, the amphibrach being a foot of three syllables, of which the middle syllable is accented:—

The gréy winds, | the cóld winds | are blówing;

and that is the predominant movement of this lyric:—

> All day I hear the noise of waters
> Making moan
> Sad as the sea-bird is when going
> Forth alone,
> He hears the winds cry to the waters'
> Monotone.
>
> The grey winds, the cold winds are blowing
> Where I go.
> I hear the noise of many waters
> Far below.
> All day, all night, I hear them flowing
> To and fro.

That poem alone refutes Miss Lowell's statement that one cannot change the rhythm of fixed verse except by abruptly jumping from one metre to another. The phrasing through that poem is amphibrachic, that is to say, the natural groups of words are likely to be amphibrachs ("of waters," "when going," "the waters") but all of the long lines do not scan as pure amphibrachs, while each short line is the opposite of an amphibrach,—being a cretic, a foot consisting of a short between two longs.

English poetry as a whole refutes Miss Lowell's idea of the invariability of rhythm when we use a fixed metric scheme. Not only can we have lyrics like the above, which, if scanned in the ordinary way, *i.e.*,—

All day | all night | I hear | them flow | ing to | and fro,

gives us straight iambic verse, yet are rhythmically quite different from it, but we can put trochaic phrasing on an iambic base. Indeed, one of the latest books on prosody, Andrews's "The Reading and Writing of Verse," devotes a whole chapter to the more obvious variations of movement and phrasing within the metric schemes.

I have said that English lyrical verse is distinguished from syllabic verse and from prose by its regularly recurring accents. Briefly noting that Miss Lowell's list of feet does not at all allow for verse in quadruple time, where there are four syllables to each foot, let us see what she has to say on the matter of free verse. To our surprise she essays to bring free verse into the fold of what has been considered regular verse in English for a good many years. Here is Miss Lowell's apologia:—

> The French word *vers* does not mean "verse" but line. [Of course, the word "verse" actually means line if we use our terms accurately.] *Vers libre,* then, meant "free line," or a line which was not obliged to contain a prescribed number of feet. Had we called the form, as the French do, "free line" we should at least have had an accurate, if exceedingly clumsy, title for it. The proper English term is really "cadenced verse"; that is, verse built upon cadence and not upon metre. By "cadence" in poetry, we mean a rhythmic curve, containing one or more stressed accents, and corresponding roughly to the necessity of breathing. This must also correspond to a depression or slight dropping in the tension of the subject at that point. These curves are made up of a number of time-units, which, again, although they do not accord perfectly, still do so with extraordinary approximation. Cadenced verse is non-syllabic, and in that sense resembles music far more than the old metrical verse ever did. As music varies the number of notes in a bar by splitting them up into smaller time-valuations, so cadenced verse may vary the number of its syllables within the duration of its time-units to any extent desired. Much cadenced verse can be read to a metronome, although the inexorable tick is certainly as annoying to the reader as it is to the musical performer, be he singer or instrumentalist.

Miss Lowell follows this paragraph with the remarks about metrical verse which I have already quoted.

First Impressions

Readers of the ordinary specimens of free verse will be surprised to learn from the above that it is more like music than the regular verse that the late Dr. Campion—for instance—used to write. But their surprise will be at least mitigated if they recognize that what Miss Lowell has described above is not free verse at all, but stress verse. Although he does not analyze it in time-units, Dr. Bridges has already written an elaborate book largely devoted to the exposition of such verse,—his "Milton's Prosody." But to expect Miss Lowell to concern herself with the work of so "academic" a theorist and a poet as Dr. Bridges would, perhaps, be too much. Her description applies to nearly all of Coleridge's "Christabel," of course—that poem and its preface being classical in this connection. It describes the stress verse written by Robert Bridges, of which this may be taken as a rather well-known example:—

LONDON SNOW [1]

When | men were | all a | sleep the | snow came | flying,
   In | large white | flakes | falling on the | city | brown,
| Stealthily and per | petually | settling and | loosely | lying
  | Hushing the | latest | traffic of the | drowsy | town. . . .

The reader will note that the number of beats in each line is constant, while the number of syllables

[1] The foot-mark is placed before each stressed syllable to show the variable number of syllables to the "foot," as we may call it for convenience.

246

is not. But this verse, though fulfilling the conditions laid down by Miss Lowell, is certainly not free verse. And it is not verse which she could consistently call metrical. What is it, then?

Apparently it is something which is not at all present to Miss Lowell's consciousness. But if her own free verse is not the same thing as the above—and one has only to read it to hear that it is not, what is it? Miss Lowell is very fond of quoting the remarks of Professor Patterson of Columbia, who studied rhythms with phonographic and time-recording apparatus, and of referring to "my experiments with Dr. Patterson." What I do not remember to have seen her quote is the result of Dr. Patterson's experiments with her, and so I shall quote them here. They occur in the preface to the second edition of his book, "The Rhythms of Prose":—

What is achieved, as a rule, in Miss Lowell's case, is emotional prose, emphatically phrased, excellent and moving. "Spaced prose" we may call it. With other writers the result is often merely unrhymed verse, with irregular length of line; or, as is frequently apparent in the writings of Edgar Lee Masters, a mosaic of bits of verse and bits of prose experience.

Miss Lowell delivers her *vers libre* with much more swing and vim than one commonly hears in prose; but surely all particularly vigorous prose, if it is to be valued as a fit medium for vigorous thought and feeling, must also be thus delivered. Colonel Roosevelt, in fact, delivers his own prose with just as much "stress" and with just as much "curve"—to use Miss Lowell's defining terms in her account of *vers libre*—as Miss Lowell contributes to her "free verse." Where, then, is the preferential difference as to form? If there is any difference in *degree* of stress, the intensity is undoubtedly more pronounced in the delivery of Colonel Roosevelt. . . .

That ought to settle the question, and I may sum up the result of the foregoing criticism as follows:—

The upholders of free verse, who are usually also the detractors of regular verse, seek to exalt their alleged form—which experiments show is not a separate form at all—by misrepresenting the constitution of ordinary verse.

They misrepresent it by confounding its metre and its rhythm, which latter is a free movement emphasized and made more measurable to the ear by being written against a metric scheme which is sometimes quite apparent or, as in the case of blank verse, is not always apparent but exists as a convention in the mind of the poet and of the auditor.

This confusion enables them to say, without any sense of unveracity, that the poets have "wrung out" of the fixed forms all that is possible, whereas the truth is that with our English accentuation, our English syllable-lengths, and the possibilities of "time" in the musical sense, and of pauses in the musical and in the grammatical senses, our regular and stress verse is capable of endless variations.

They write—often—stress or regular verse without knowing it, and when they find that their real free verse is actually prose they hasten to cover it with the mantle (with the previous owner's name-tag removed) of stress-prosody, a form as old as the earliest modern English verse, but one which, under French syllabic-prosody influence, simply failed of recognition for a few generations.

The result of this metrical propaganda, in which others besides Miss Lowell have indulged, is that young poets who might otherwise be trying to carry on the "free" tradition in English verse, who might be experimenting both along the lines laid down by Bridges for stress-verse and along those laid down by Stone for verse that is quantitative in the classical sense, are, instead, writing in a mixture which has no rhythmical foundation and which generally fails to be musical or pleasing, and sometimes even fails to be expressive at all.

THE END